## CAMBRIDGE
## UNIVERSITY PRESS

# CAMBRIDGE
# Primary Mathematics

## Workbook 5

Mary Wood & Emma Low

# CAMBRIDGE
## UNIVERSITY PRESS

University Printing House, Cambridge CB2 8BS, United Kingdom

One Liberty Plaza, 20th Floor, New York, NY 10006, USA

477 Williamstown Road, Port Melbourne, VIC 3207, Australia

314–321, 3rd Floor, Plot 3, Splendor Forum, Jasola District Centre, New Delhi – 110025, India

79 Anson Road, #06–04/06, Singapore 079906

Cambridge University Press is part of the University of Cambridge.

It furthers the University's mission by disseminating knowledge in the pursuit of education, learning and research at the highest international levels of excellence.

www.cambridge.org
Information on this title: www.cambridge.org/9781108746311

© Cambridge University Press 2021

First published 2014

Second edition 2021

20 19 18 17 16 15 14 13 12 11 10 9 8 7 6 5 4 3 2

Printed in Italy by L.E.G.O. S.p.A.

A catalogue record for this publication is available from the British Library

ISBN 978-1-108-74631-1 Paperback with Digital Access (1 Year)

Additional resources for this publication at www.cambridge.org/9781108746311

# Contents

# Contents

# How to use this book

This workbook provides questions for you to practise what you have learned in class. There is a unit to match each unit in your Learner's Book. Each exercise is divided into three parts:

- **Focus:** these questions help you to master the basics

- **Practice:** these questions help you to become more confident in using what you have learned

- **Challenge:** these questions will make you think very hard.

You might not need to work on all three parts of each exercise. Your teacher will tell you which parts to do.

You will also find these features:

Important words that you will use. ———→

| decimal | hundredth |
|---|---|
| decimal place | place value |
| decimal point | tenth |

Step-by-step examples showing a way to solve a problem. ————————→

*There are often many different ways to solve a problem.*

**Worked example 1**

Mai, Yared and Susan live in different time zones.

The time on Yared's clock is 2 hours ahead of the time on Mai's clock.

The time on Susan's clock is 3 hours behind the time on Mai's clock.

The time in Mai's time zone is 15:07. What is the time for Yared and Susan?

| | |
|---|---|
| Yared's time is 2 hours ahead of Mai's. | Add 2 hours to 15:07. |
| The time for Yared is 17:07. | |
| Susan's time is 3 hours behind Mai's. | Subtract 3 hours from 15:07. |
| The time for Susan is 12:07. | |

These questions will help ————→ you develop your skills of thinking and working mathematically.

**11** Draw a ring around the odd one out.

368.4 tenths     368.4     3684 hundredths

36.84     368 tenths and 4 hundredths

Explain your answer.

_____

# Thinking and Working Mathematically

There are some important skills that you will develop as you learn mathematics.

**Specialising**
is when I choose an example and check to see if it satisfies or does not satisfy specific mathematical criteria.

**Characterising**
is when I identify and describe the mathematical properties of an object.

**Generalising**
is when I recognise an underlying pattern by identifying many examples that satisfy the same mathematical criteria.

**Classifying**
is when I organise objects into groups according to their mathematical properties.

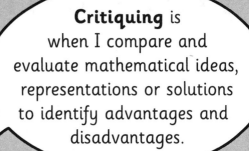

**Critiquing** is when I compare and evaluate mathematical ideas, representations or solutions to identify advantages and disadvantages.

**Improving** is when I refine mathematical ideas or representations to develop a more effective approach or solution.

**Conjecturing** is when I form mathematical questions or ideas.

**Convincing** is when I present evidence to justify or challenge a mathematical idea or solution.

# 1 The number system

## > 1.1 Understanding place value

**Worked example 1**

Find the missing numbers.

**a** $0.9 \times \boxed{\phantom{00}} = 9$

**b** $350 \div \boxed{\phantom{00}} = 3.5$

<table>
<tr><td>compose</td><td>decimal point</td></tr>
<tr><td>decimal</td><td>hundredth</td></tr>
<tr><td>decimal place</td><td>place value</td></tr>
<tr><td>decompose</td><td>tenth</td></tr>
</table>

**a**

| 100s | 10s | 1s | $\frac{1}{10}$s | $\frac{1}{100}$s |
|------|-----|----|----|-----|
|  |  | 0 | 9 |  |
|  |  | 9 |  |  |

$0.9 \times 10 = 9$

Use a place value grid to help you.

To move digits one column to the left you multiply by 10.

**b**

| 100s | 10s | 1s | $\frac{1}{10}$s | $\frac{1}{100}$s |
|------|-----|----|----|-----|
| 3 | 5 | 0 |  |  |
|  |  | 3 | 5 | 0 |

$350 \div 100 = 3.5$

To move digits two columns to the right you divide by 100.

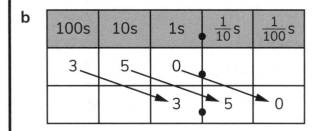

# Exercise 1.1

## Focus

1   Write the missing numbers in this sequence.

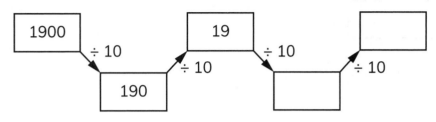

> **Tip**
>
> You may find a place value grid helpful for these questions.

2   Write these numbers in digits.

a   fifteen point three seven                          _____

b   one hundred and five point zero five    _____

c   thirty four point three four                      _____

3   Write the missing numbers.

a

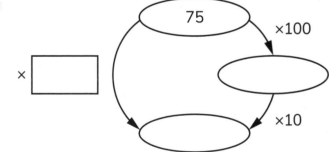

b

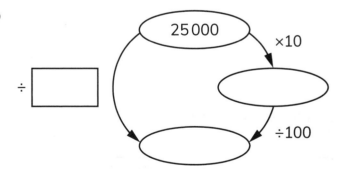

4  Complete the table to show what the digits in the number 47.56 stand for.

| 4 | tens |
|---|------|
| 5 |      |
| 6 |      |
| 7 |      |

5  Write the missing number.

$6.58 = 6 + \boxed{\phantom{xxx}} + 0.08$

**Practice**

6  Draw a ring around the number equivalent to five hundredths.

500          5.00          0.50          0.05

7  Divide 3.6 by 10.

_____

8  Write the missing numbers.

$38.14 = 30 + 8 + \boxed{\phantom{xxx}} + \boxed{\phantom{xxx}}$

9  Regroup 30.54 in two different ways.

1  _____

2  _____

10  Here are four number cards.

Draw a ring round the card that shows the number that is 100 times bigger than 33.3.

| 33.300 |   | 3330 |   | 333.00 |   | 33300 |
|--------|---|------|---|--------|---|-------|

11 Find the missing numbers.

    a  $7.2 \times 100 =$ ☐    b  $0.75 \times 100 =$ ☐    c  $4.28 \times 10 =$ ☐

    d  $270 \div 100 =$ ☐    e  $151 \div 100 =$ ☐    f  $6.6 \div 10 =$ ☐

 12 Draw a ring around the odd one out.

       368.4 tenths       368.4       3684 hundredths

         36.84       368 tenths and 4 hundredths

Explain your answer.

_____

## Challenge

13 Write down the value of the digit 3 in each of these numbers.

    a  72.3  _____

    b  eighty-four point zero three  _____

 14 Arun has these cards.

        | 2 | 3 | 5 | • |

Write **all** the numbers he can make between 0 and 40 using all four cards.

_____

_____

15 Write the missing numbers.

    a  ☐ $\times 0.6 = 6$        b  $103 \div$ ☐ $= 1.03$

    c  ☐ $\times 0.13 = 13$      d  $76 \div$ ☐ $= 7.6$

    e  ☐ $\times 4.1 = 410$      f  $0.09 \times$ ☐ $= 9$

16 Look at this number line.
   Write the number that goes in the box.

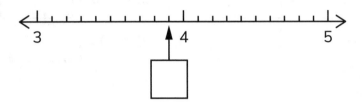

17 Heidi makes cakes for a snack bar.

   a  It costs $1.50 to make one chocolate cake.

      How much does it cost to make 100 chocolate cakes?

      _____

   b  It costs $19.00 to make 100 small cakes.

      How much does it cost to make 10 small cakes?

      _____

   c  It costs $0.75 to make a sponge cake.

      How much does it cost to make 100 sponge cakes?

      _____

 18 Arun and Marcus each write a decimal number between zero
   and one.

   Arun says, 'My number has 9 hundredths and Marcus's
   number has only 7 hundredths so my number must be bigger.'

   Arun is not correct. Explain why.

   _____

   _____

   _____

   _____

# > 1.2 Rounding decimal numbers

**Worked example 2**

A number with 1 decimal place is rounded to the nearest whole number.

a    What is the smallest number that rounds to 10?

b    What is the largest number that rounds to 20?

nearest

round

round to the nearest

---

You can use a number line to help you.

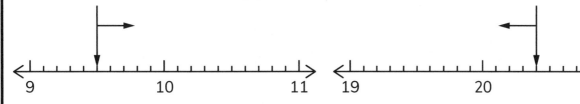

a    9.5

b    20.4

If the tenths digit is 5, 6, 7, 8 or 9 the number rounds up to the nearest whole number.

If the tenths digit is 0, 1, 2, 3 or 4 the number rounds down to the nearest whole number.

## Exercise 1.2

**Focus**

1    Here is part of a number line. The arrow shows the position of a number.

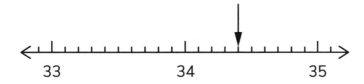

Complete the sentence for this number.

_____ rounded to the nearest whole number is _____ .

2  Zara has four number cards.

| 36.5 | 35.4 | 36.4 | 35.1 |

She rounds each number to the nearest whole number.

Which of her numbers rounds to 36?

_____

3  Draw a line to match each number to the nearest whole number on the number line.

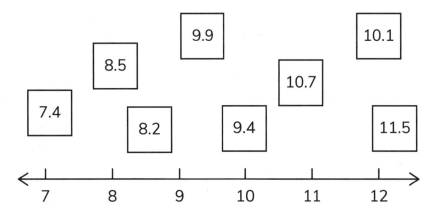

 4  Write a number with 1 decimal place to complete each number sentence.

_____ rounds to 1

_____ rounds to 10

**Practice**

5  Round these lengths to the nearest whole centimetre.

a   4.1 cm  _____ cm               b   6.6 cm  _____ cm

c   10.1 cm  _____ cm              d   8.5 cm  _____ cm

6   Here are three number cards.

Use each card once to make a number that rounds to 20 to the nearest whole number.

☐☐.☐

7   A number with 1 decimal place is rounded to the nearest whole number.

a   What is the smallest number that rounds to 100?

_____

b   What is the largest number that rounds to 100?

_____

## Challenge

8   Write the letters of all the numbers that round to 10 to the nearest whole number. What word is spelt out?

| A | B | C | D | E | F | G | H | I | J | K | L | M |
|------|------|-----|------|------|-----|-----|-----|------|-----|------|-----|------|
| 10.8 | 10.1 | 9.3 | 11.1 | 10.4 | 7.8 | 8.8 | 9.3 | 19.8 | 1.9 | 10.7 | 9.6 | 99.9 |

| N | O | P | Q | R | S | T | U | V | W | X | Y | Z |
|-----|-----|------|-----|------|-----|-----|------|------|------|------|-----|-----|
| 1.8 | 9.2 | 10.6 | 9.1 | 10.5 | 7.9 | 9.5 | 19.9 | 16.2 | 10.9 | 20.3 | 8.9 | 9.4 |

_____

9 Here are eight numbers.

19.4   19.9   21.1   20.4   20.3   19.7   21.4   10.1

Draw a ring round the number that these clues are describing.

- The number rounds to 20 to the nearest whole number.

- The tenths digit is odd.

- The sum of the digits is less than 18.

- The tens digit is even.

 10 Rashid has these number cards.

| 1.4 | 2.4 | 3.4 | 4.4 |

He chooses two cards.

He adds the numbers on the cards together.

He rounds the result to the nearest whole number.

His answer is 7.

Which two cards did he choose?

_____ and _____ .

 11 Arun rounds these numbers to the nearest whole number.

3.3   3.5   3.7   3.9   4.4   4.5   4.9

He sorts them into 3 groups and places them in a table.

Complete the table.

| Rounds to _____ | Rounds to _____ | Rounds to _____ |
|---|---|---|
|  |  |  |

# 2 ▸ 2D shape and pattern

## ❯ 2.1 Triangles

**Worked example 1**

Is this triangle isosceles?

> equilateral triangle
>
> isosceles triangle
>
> scalene triangle

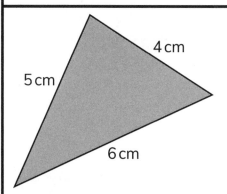

Measure the length of each side of the triangle.

In an isosceles triangle, two sides have the same length.

The sides are all different lengths.

**Answer:** No, the triangle is not isosceles.

# Exercise 2.1

**Focus**

 1   Is this triangle isosceles?

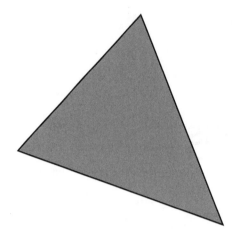

How do you know?

_____

_____

 2   Draw a ring around the scalene triangles.

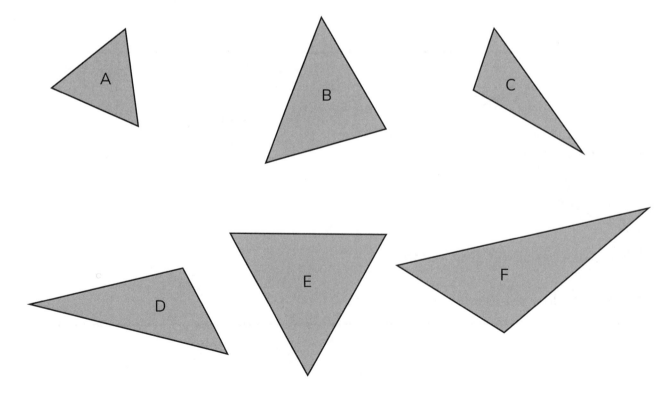

3   Label the angle at each vertex of these triangles 'acute',
    'obtuse' or 'right angle'.

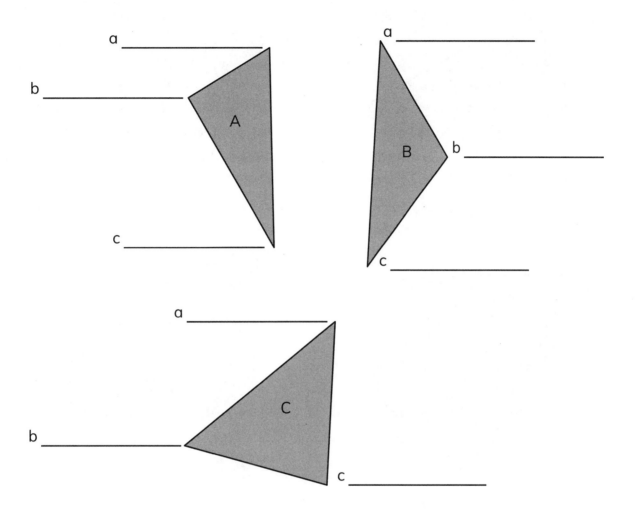

a _____

b _____

A

c _____

a _____

b _____

B

c _____

a _____

b _____

C

c _____

**Practice**

4   Draw a scalene triangle using a ruler and pencil.

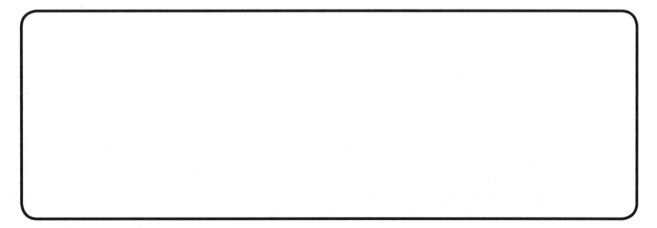

5   On each of these isosceles triangles, circle the angles that are the same
    size. You could use tracing paper to compare the sizes of the angles.

a

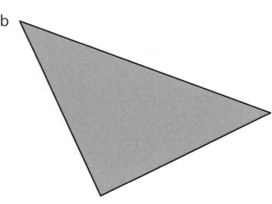

b

c

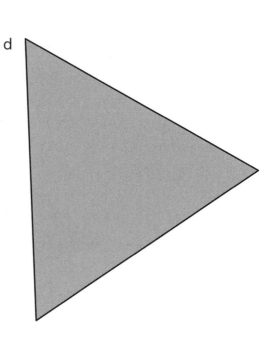

d

6   a   Write a sentence about the sides of an equilateral triangle.

    _____

    _____

    b   Write a sentence about the angles of an equilateral triangle.

    _____

    _____

**Challenge**

7 a Draw an isosceles triangle with two sides 6 cm long and the
other side shorter than 6 cm.

b Draw an isosceles triangle with two sides 6 cm long and the
other side longer than 6 cm.

8   Trace the triangles in this tessellating pattern.
    Make templates of the triangles and complete the pattern.

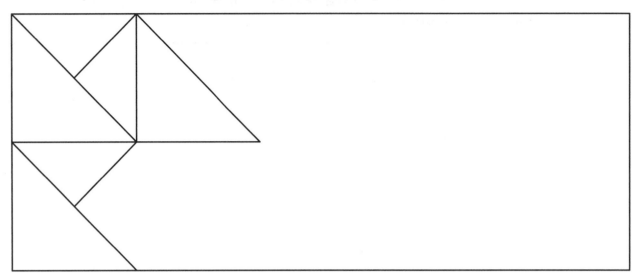

9   This is a crossword. It is filled in with words about triangles.
    Write the clues for the crossword.

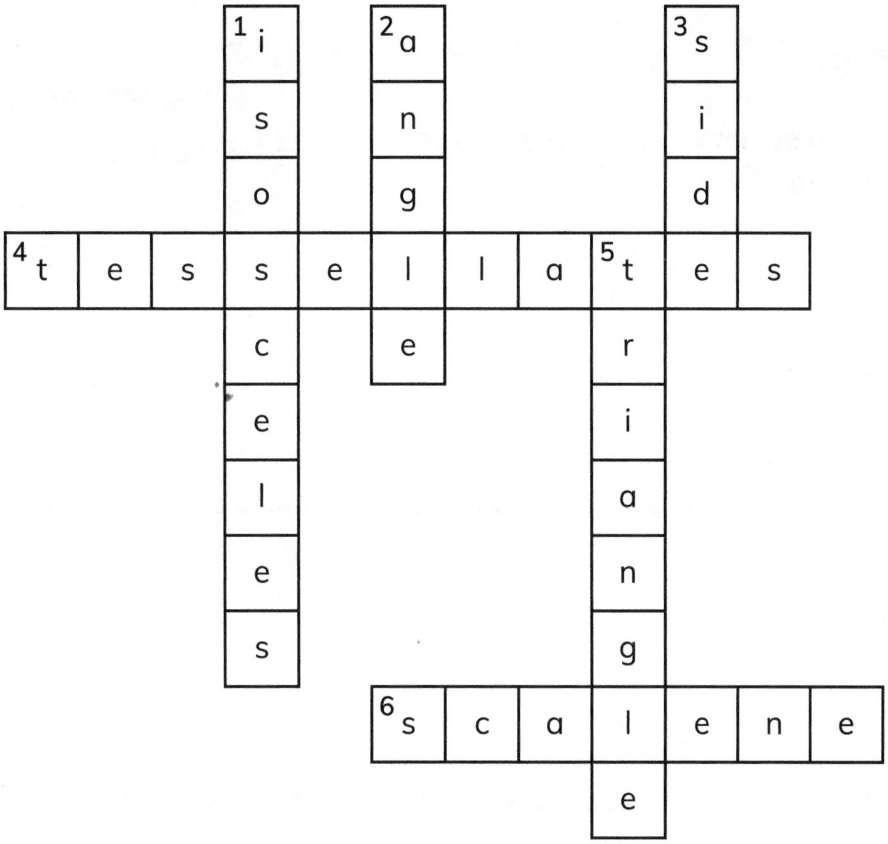

Across →

4 _____

6 _____

Down ↓

1 _____

2 _____

3 _____

5 _____

# > 2.2 Symmetry

**Worked example 2**

Colour the squares to make a symmetrical pattern where the dashed line is a line of symmetry.

line of symmetry

symmetrical

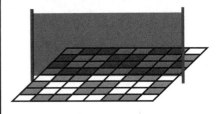

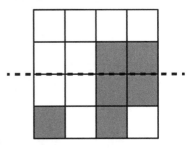

Place a small mirror along the mirror line to see what the complete symmetrical pattern will look like.

Reflect the shaded squares across the mirror line.

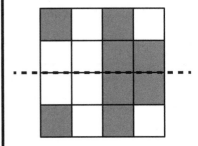

Squares that are next to the mirror line are reflected to squares that are next to the mirror line on the other side.

Squares that are one square away from the mirror line are reflected to squares that are one square away from the mirror line on the other side.

**Answer:**

# Exercise 2.2

## Focus

1  Spot the difference.
   Draw shapes on the right side of the
   picture to make it a reflection of
   the picture on the left.

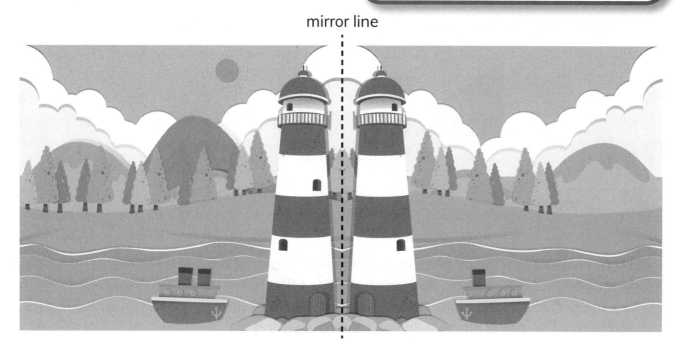

2  Zara says that she is thinking of a triangle with three lines
   of symmetry. Draw a ring around the name of the triangle
   that Zara is thinking of.

   scalene          isosceles          equilateral

3  Shade squares to make a pattern with one line of symmetry.

mirror line

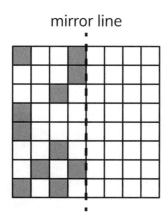

4   Predict where the reflection of the triangle will be after it is reflected over each of the mirror lines. Draw your predictions using a ruler.

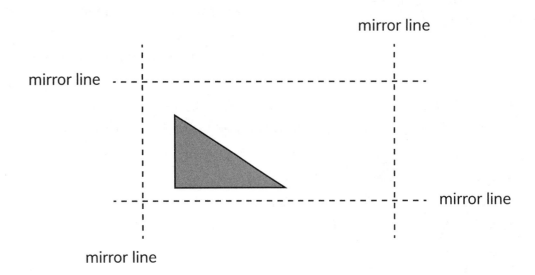

Check your predictions by placing a mirror along each of the mirror lines in turn. Look at how the triangle is reflected.
Tick the predicted reflections that are correct. Use a different colour pencil to correct the predictions that are wrong.

**Practice**

5   Use a ruler to draw all of the lines of symmetry on these triangles.

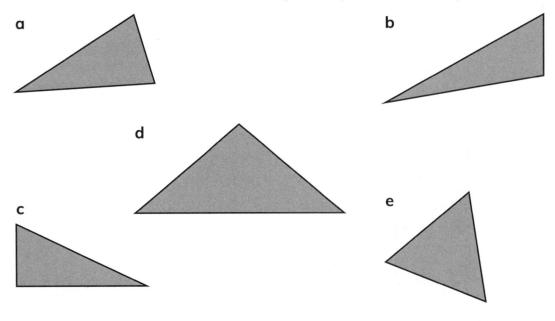

a

b

d

c

e

6   Shade 5 squares in each of the empty quadrants to make a pattern with two lines of symmetry.

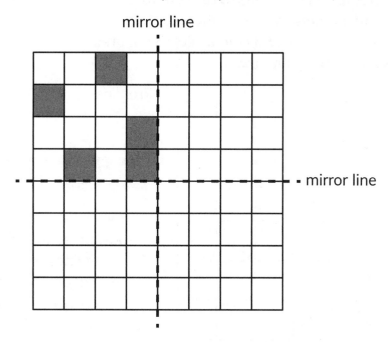

7   Reflect the square, triangle, rectangle and pentagon over both the horizontal and vertical mirror lines until you make a pattern with reflective symmetry.

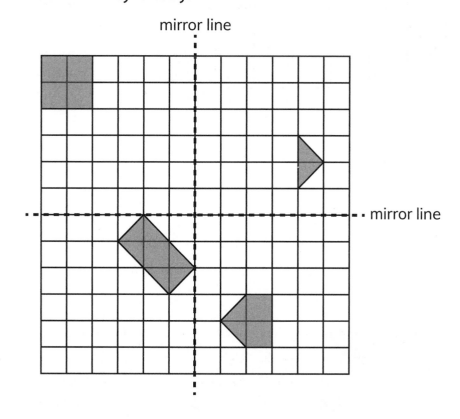

**Challenge**

8  Choose four different coloured pencils or pens. Use them to shade in the squares and half squares marked with a star (*). Reflect the pattern over the mirror lines and colour all the squares to make a pattern with two lines of symmetry.

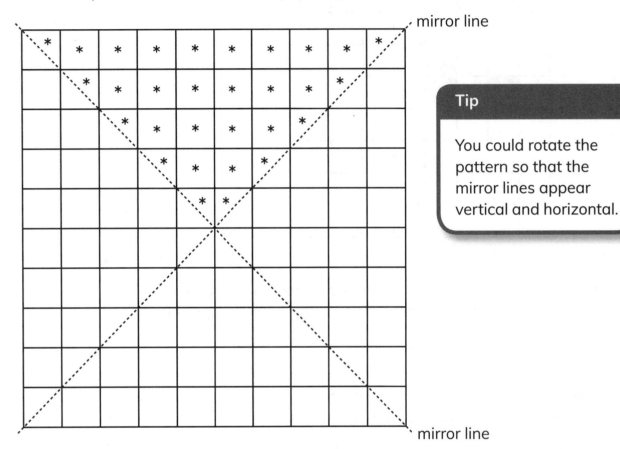

mirror line

mirror line

**Tip**

You could rotate the pattern so that the mirror lines appear vertical and horizontal.

9   This is a chessboard.

a   How many lines of symmetry does a
    chessboard have?

    _____

b   Where could you place a counter on the
    chessboard so that the chessboard still has
    two lines of symmetry?
    Mark the place with a circle.

c   Where could you place a counter on the
    chessboard so that the chessboard has no
    lines of symmetry?
    Mark the place with a cross.

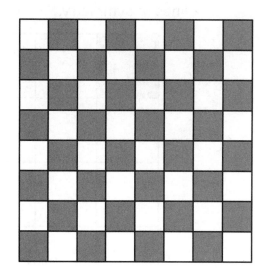

d   Where could you place a counter on the chessboard
    so that the chessboard has only one line
    of symmetry?
    Mark the place with a triangle.

10 a   Colour two more squares so that this pattern has exactly
       1 line of symmetry.

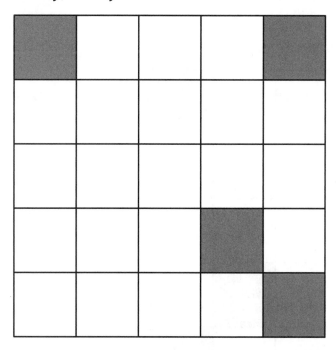

b   Colour two more squares so that this pattern has exactly
    2 lines of symmetry.

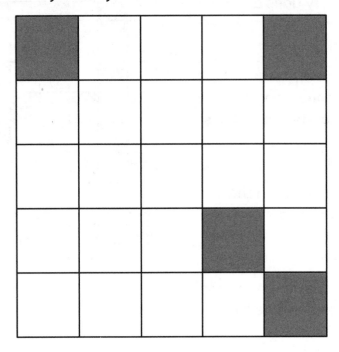

c   What is the fewest number of squares that have to be shaded
    to make this pattern have exactly 4 lines of symmetry?

_____

Shade the grid to show your solution.

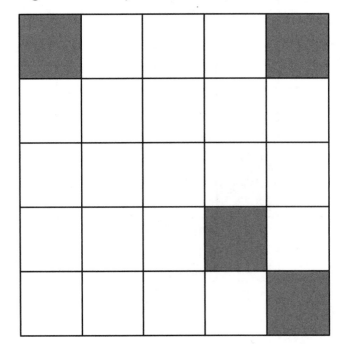

# 3 > Numbers and sequences

## > 3.1 Counting and sequences

| linear sequence |
| sequence |
| term |
| term-to-term rule |

Six jumps of 8 is 48 so after counting back six lots of 8 Marcus says the number 2.

The next number Marcus says is −6.

Another way to think about this question is:

Each term is 2 more than a multiple of 8.

10 is 2 more than a multiple of 8 and if you count back in 8s you get to 10, then 2 and then −6.

**Answer:** −6

## Exercise 3.1

**Focus**

1   What is the next number in this sequence?

8, 6, 4, 2, 0, ...

How do you know?

2   This is an 8 by 8 number grid.

| 1 | 2 | 3 | 4 | 5 | 6 | 7 | 8 |
|---|---|---|---|---|---|---|---|
| 9 | 10 | 11 | 12 | 13 | 14 | 15 | 16 |
| 17 | 18 | 19 | 20 | 21 | 22 | 23 | 24 |
| 25 | 26 | 27 | 28 | 29 | 30 | 31 | 32 |
| 33 | 34 | 35 | 36 | 37 | 38 | 39 | 40 |
| 41 | 42 | 43 | 44 | 45 | 46 | 47 | 48 |
| 49 | 50 | 51 | 52 | 53 | 54 | 55 | 56 |
| 57 | 58 | 59 | 60 | 61 | 62 | 63 | 64 |

a   Colour the multiples of 7.

b   What do you notice?

_____

c   If you continued the sequence would 100 be in it?

_____

3   This pattern makes a sequence.

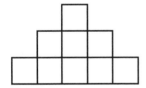

You count the squares in each row of the staircase.

The sequence starts 1, 3, 5, ...

a   Complete the table.

| Row number | 1 | 2 | 3 | 4 | 5 | 6 | 7 |
|---|---|---|---|---|---|---|---|
| Number of squares in row | 1 | 3 | 5 | | | | |

b   Continue the sequence to show your results.

1, 3, 5, _____ , _____ , _____ , _____ , _____ , _____

c   What is the term-to-term rule for the sequence?

_____

## Practice

4   A sequence starts at 19.

9 is subtracted each time.

What is the first number in the sequence that is less than zero?

_____

5   Zara counts back in steps of equal size.

Write the missing numbers in her sequence.

_____ , _____ , 61, 52, _____ , 34

6   a   Here are some patterns made from sticks.
Draw the next pattern in the sequence.

    1                 2                        3

b   Complete the table.

| Pattern number | Number of sticks |
|:---:|:---:|
| 1 | |
| 2 | |
| 3 | |
| 4 | |

c   Find the term-to-term rule.

_____

d  How many sticks are in the 10th pattern?

_____

7  A sequence starts at 400 and 90 is added each time.

400,    490,    580,    670, ...

What is the first number in the sequence that is greater than 1000?

_____

## Challenge

8  a  Draw the next pattern in the sequence.

 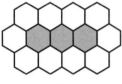 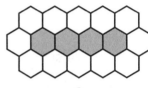

1            2            3

b  Complete the table.

| Pattern number | Number of hexagons |
|:---:|:---:|
| 1 | |
| 2 | |
| 3 | |
| 4 | |

c  Find the term-to-term rule.

_____

d  How many hexagons are in the 8th pattern?

_____

**9** Sofia counts in threes starting at 3.

$$3, \quad 6, \quad 9, \quad 12, ...$$

Zara counts in fives starting at 5.

$$5, \quad 10, \quad 15, \quad 20, ...$$

They both count on.

What is the **first** number greater than 100 that both Sofia and Zara say?

_____

Explain your answer.

_____

_____

**10** Zara writes a sequence of five numbers.

The first number is 2.

The last number is 18.

Her rule is to add the same amount each time.

Write the missing numbers.

$$2, \underline{\hspace{1.5cm}}, \underline{\hspace{1.5cm}}, \underline{\hspace{1.5cm}}, 18$$

**11** Arun writes a sequence of numbers.

His rule is to add the same amount each time.

Write the missing numbers.

$$-1, \underline{\hspace{1.5cm}}, \underline{\hspace{1.5cm}}, 14$$

# > 3.2 Square and triangular numbers

**Worked example 2**

Look at these patterns made from squares.

The sequence starts 1, 3, 6, ...

**a** Draw the next term in the sequence.

**b** Write the next three numbers in the sequence.

---

**a**

Each term has an extra column that is one square taller.

**b** 10, 15, 21

The sequence 1, 3, 6, 10, 15, 21, ... is the sequence of triangular numbers.

---

spatial pattern

square number

triangular number

## Exercise 3.2

**Focus**

1 Draw the next term in this sequence.

What is the mathematical name for these numbers?

_____

2  Draw the next term in this sequence.

What is the mathematical name for these numbers?

_____

3  Write the next two terms in these sequences.

a  1, 4, 9, 16, 25, _____ , _____

b  1, 3, 6, 10, _____ , _____

## Practice

4  This pattern is made by adding two consecutive triangular numbers.

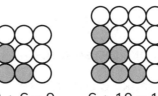

1      1 + 3 = 4      3 + 6 = 9      6 + 10 = 16

> **Tip**
>
> Remember that consecutive means next to each other.

a  Look at the total in each term and complete this sentence.

The terms in the sequence are the _____ numbers.

b  Write the next two calculations complete with their answers.

_____          _____

5  Find the value of $8^2$.

_____

**6** Solve these number riddles.

   a   The number is:

- a square number

- a multiple of 3

- less than 25    _____

   b   The number is:

- a square number

- an even number

- a single digit number    _____

   c   The number is:

- a square number

- a 2-digit number

- the sum of the digits is 13    _____

 **7** Zara has a lot of small squares all equal in size.

She uses the small squares to make big squares.

She can use 9 small squares to make a big square.

   a   Which of these numbers of squares could Zara use to make a big square?

| 46 | 64 | 14 | 4 | 24 | 100 |
|----|----|----|----|----|-----|
| 60 | 66 | 18 | 81 | 9 | 90 |

_____

   b   Can Zara make a big square using 49 small squares?

Explain how you know.

_____

_____

**Challenge**

8   Write the missing numbers in the table.

| Product of two numbers | 1 more than the product | Equivalent square number |
|---|---|---|
| $1 \times 3 = 3$ | 4 | $2^2 = 4$ |
| $2 \times 4 = 8$ | 9 | $3^2 = 9$ |
| $3 \times 5 = 15$ | ☐ | $☐^2 = ☐$ |
| $4 \times 6 = ☐$ | ☐ | $☐^2 = ☐$ |
| $☐ \times ☐ = ☐$ | ☐ | $☐^2 = ☐$ |

**Tip**

Remember that each row continues the pattern.

9   Find two square numbers to make each of these calculations correct.

a   ☐ + ☐ = 10          b   ☐ + ☐ = 20

c   ☐ + ☐ = 40          d   ☐ + ☐ = 50

e   ☐ + ☐ = 80          f   ☐ + ☐ = 90

g   ☐ + ☐ = 100

10  Find the 10th term in this sequence.

1, 3, 6, 10, 15, _____

# > 3.3 Prime and composite numbers

**Worked example 3**

Here are four digit cards.

| 3 | 9 | 2 | 1 |

Use each card once to make two 2-digit prime numbers.

[ ][ ] and [ ][ ]

> composite number
>
> factor
>
> multiple
>
> prime number

The prime numbers are:

2, 3, 5, 7, 11, 13, 17, 19, 23, 29, 31, 37, ...    Start by writing a list of prime numbers.

**Answer:** 13 and 29

Choose two of these numbers that satisfy the criteria.

You could also have chosen

      31 and 29

or    19 and 23

There is more than one correct answer.

You are **specialising** when you choose a number and check whether it satisfies the criteria.

# Exercise 3.3

**Focus**

1   Here is a grid of numbers.

Shade all the prime numbers. What letter is revealed?

| 14 | 2 | 13 | 5 | 8 |
|----|----|----|----|----|
| 15 | 3 | 1 | 11 | 15 |
| 1 | 11 | 19 | 7 | 6 |
| 9 | 17 | 9 | 15 | 12 |
| 12 | 5 | 16 | 4 | 14 |

2   Write each number in the correct place on the diagram.

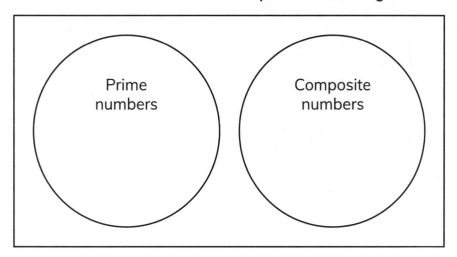

2, 3, 4, 5, 6

3   Complete this sentence.

A number with only two factors is called a _____ number.

**Practice**

4   Here is a grid of numbers.

Draw a path between the two shaded numbers that passes **only** through prime numbers.

You must **not** move diagonally.

| 2 | 4 | 6 | 8 | 13 |
|---|---|---|---|----|
| 3 | 23 | 29 | 71 | 65 |
| 1 | 51 | 45 | 7 | 5 |
| 15 | 92 | 25 | 1 | 2 |
| 31 | 37 | 16 | 14 | 11 |

5   a   Find two different prime numbers that total 9.

[   ] + [   ] = 9

b   Find two different prime numbers that total 50.

[   ] + [   ] = 50

6   Show that 15 is a composite number.

_____

**Challenge**

7   Use the clues to find two prime numbers less than 20.

Prime number 1: Subtracting 4 from this prime number gives a multiple of 5.

Prime number 2: This prime number is one more than a multiple of 4, but not 1 less than a multiple of 3.

Prime number 1 is _____          Prime number 2 is _____

8 Multiples of 6 are shaded on this grid.

| 1 | 2 | 3 | 4 | 5 | 6 | 7 | 8 | 9 | 10 |
|---|---|---|---|---|---|---|---|---|----|
| 11 | 12 | 13 | 14 | 15 | 16 | 17 | 18 | 19 | 20 |
| 21 | 22 | 23 | | | 27 | 28 | | 30 | |

Ingrid looks at the grid and says, 'One more than any multiple of 6 is always a prime number.'

Ingrid is wrong.

Explain how you know.

_____

_____

9 Arun chooses a prime number.

He rounds it to the nearest 10 and his answer is 70.

Write all the possible prime numbers Arun could choose.

_____

 10 Write each whole number from 1 to 20 in the correct place on this Venn diagram.

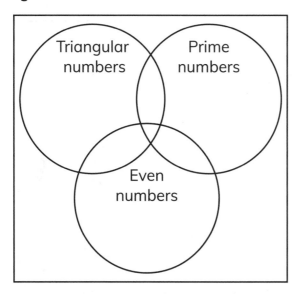

# 4 Averages

## > 4.1 Mode and median

### Worked example 1

What is the mode of these areas?

$45 \, cm^2$, $36 \, cm^2$, $18 \, cm^2$, $36 \, cm^2$, $21 \, cm^2$, $45 \, cm^2$, $36 \, cm^2$

| | |
|---|---|
| One area is $18 \, cm^2$ | Count how many there are of each area. |
| One area is $21 \, cm^2$ | The mode is the area that appears the most often. |
| Three areas are $36 \, cm^2$ | |
| Two areas are $45 \, cm^2$ | |

**Answer:** The mode is $36 \, cm^2$.

## Exercise 4.1

**Focus**

1   This box contains some numbers.

   a   How many 3s are in the box?

   b   How many 4s are in the box?

   c   What is the mode of the numbers in the box?

2   a   Write these numbers in order from smallest to greatest.

117   109   120   118   121

_____

   b   Draw a ring around the middle number.

What is the median of the numbers?  ☐

3   Complete the sentences about this set of numbers.

20    21    22    23    24    24    25

   a   The mode (most frequent) is _____ .

   b   The median (middle) is _____ .

4   This is how many sweets Tom found in each packet.

11          11          11          12          13          14          14

Complete the sentences about the average number of sweets
in a packet.

   a   The mode is _____ .

   b   The median is _____ .

## Practice

5   Explain in words how to find the median of a set of data.

First _____

Then _____

6 Tick the sets of numbers that have a mode of 8 and a median of 9.

A   10, 7, 9, 8, 11, 8, 12                     ☐

B   8, 9, 8, 10, 8, 12, 8                       ☐

C   10, 8, 8, 9, 10, 9, 10                      ☐

D   11, 8, 8, 7, 9, 10, 7, 10, 10, 8, 8, 11, 11   ☐

7 Write your own set of numbers that has a mode of 8 and a median of 9.

☐ ☐ ☐ ☐ ☐ ☐ ☐

8 Seven children reviewed a book about dinosaurs. They gave the book a score out of 5.

These are the scores.

4   1   3   5   5   1   1

a   What is the mode of the scores?

☐

b   What is the median of the scores?

☐

c   Would you use the mode or the median to describe the scores? Why?

_____

_____

**Challenge**

9 Write one more number in each set to make the statement true.

a The mode is 10.

11    10    10    11    ☐

b The mode is 4.

1    4    2    4    2    3    ☐

c The mode is **not** 31.

31    30    33    29    ☐

d The mode is **not** 108.

108    106    109    108    107    106    110    ☐

e Write three different numbers that could be added to this set of numbers to make the mode 8:

4    3    8    8    2    4    8    9    ☐

4    3    8    8    2    4    8    9    ☐

4    3    8    8    2    4    8    9    ☐

**10 a** Write five numbers that have a mode of 3 and a median of 4.

☐ ☐ ☐ ☐ ☐

**b** Write two more sets of five numbers that have a mode of 3 and a median of 4.

☐ ☐ ☐ ☐ ☐

☐ ☐ ☐ ☐ ☐

**c** What is the same about each of your sets of numbers?

_____

_____

**11** Try to write three numbers where the mode is 3 and the median is 4.

☐ ☐ ☐

Explain why it is not possible to write three numbers where the mode is 3 and the median is 4.

_____

_____

_____

_____

# 5 ▶ Addition and subtraction

## > 5.1 Addition and subtraction including decimal numbers

carry, carrying

symbol

**Worked example 1**

Calculate 2.78 − 1.94.

| | |
|---|---|
| Estimate: 3 − 2 = 1 | Always start by estimating. |
| **Method 1** | |
| 2 + 0.7 + 0.08 <br> − 1 + 0.9 + 0.04 | Decompose each number into ones, tenths and hundredths. |
| 1 + 1.7 + 0.08 <br> − 1 + 0.9 + 0.04 | You need to regroup to subtract the tenths. <br> Subtract each column then regroup to give the final answer. |
| 0 + 0.8 + 0.04 = 0.84 | |
| **Method 2** <br> 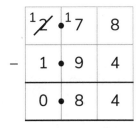 | Write the calculation in columns. <br> Use an efficient, column method. |

**Answer:** 2.78 − 1.94 = 0.84

# Exercise 5.1

**Focus**

1   Draw lines to join every pair of numbers that total 1.

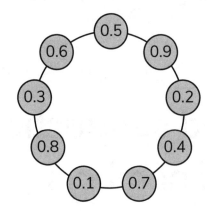

2   Join pairs of numbers that total 10.

3.7

2.4

3.4

5.8

4.2

5.4

6.3

7.6

7.3

3   Write the missing numbers.

a   4.9 + 3.5 = ☐

b   9.4 − 3.5 = ☐

4   Write the **same** number in both boxes to complete this calculation.

☐ + ☐ = 1

**Practice**

5   Write the missing numbers.

a   8.58 + 2.91 = ☐          b   7.82 − 4.49 = ☐

6   Write the missing number.

10 − ☐ = 3.45

7   Ali, Ben and Carlos calculate 9.2 − 4.7 using different methods.

**Ali's method**

Estimate: 9 − 5 = 4

9.2 − 4.7

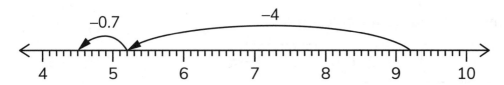

**Answer:** 4.5

**Ben's method**

Estimate: 9 − 5 = 4

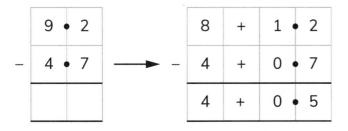

| 9 | • | 2 |
|---|---|---|
| − 4 | • | 7 |
| | | |

| 8 | + | 1 | • | 2 |
|---|---|---|---|---|
| − 4 | + | 0 | • | 7 |
| 4 | + | 0 | • | 5 |

**Answer:** 4.5

**Carlos's method**

Estimate: 9 − 5 = 4

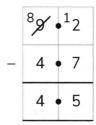

| ⁸9̸ | •¹2 |
|---|---|
| − 4 | • 7 |
| 4 | • 5 |

**Answer:** 4.5

Whose method do you like best? Explain your answer.

_____

_____

8   Sofia makes designs using hexagons and small triangles.

She gives each shape a value.

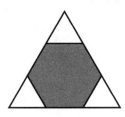

Total value 11

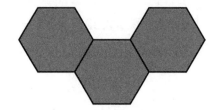

Total value 15

Find the value of a small triangle.

_____

**Challenge**

 9   Here are four digit cards.

| 8 | 4 | 2 | 5 |

Use each card once to complete the calculation.

0 . ☐☐ + 0 . ☐☐ = 1

10  Each side of a number balance has the same answer.

Write the missing number in the box to complete the number balance.

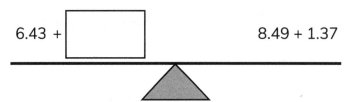

6.43 + ☐                    8.49 + 1.37

11  Write the missing digits to make the calculation correct.

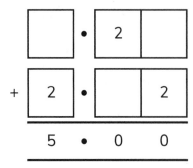

12 Use all the numbers: 0.1, 0.2, 0.3, 0.5, 0.7, 0.8, 0.9 to make the total of each line 1.5.

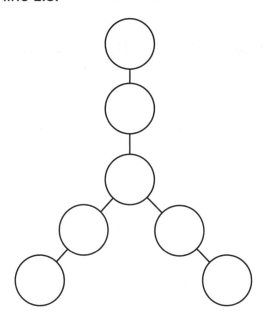

13 Kate and Heidi each buy some fruit.

Kate's fruit:

Total cost 90 cents

Heidi's fruit:

Total cost 70 cents

How much does a banana cost?

_____

## > 5.2 Addition and subtraction of positive and negative numbers

**Worked example 2**

Calculate −4 + 3.

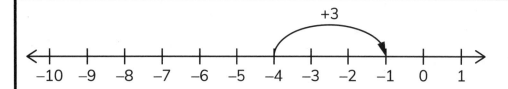

Start at −4 and count on 3.

**Answer:** −1

## Exercise 5.2

**Focus**

> integer
>
> negative number
>
> positive number

1  Complete these calculations.

a  −3 − 5 = ☐

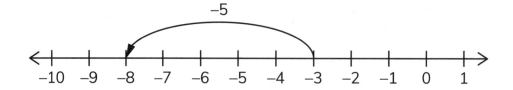

b  4 − 5 = ☐

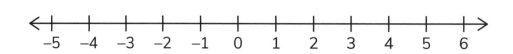

c  −9 + 3 = ☐

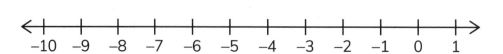

Use the number line to help you answer the rest of the questions in this exercise.

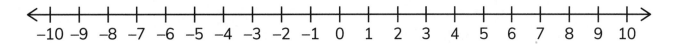

2   a   What is 4 less than 2?

_____

b   What is 3 more than −1?

_____

3   Complete these calculations.

a   −5 + 1 = ☐

b   1 − 7 = ☐

c   −2 + 5 = ☐

**Practice**

4   Calculate.

a   379 + 287 + 154

_____

b   357 + 19 + 3579

_____

5   Zara makes a sequence of numbers starting at 100.

She subtracts 45 each time.

Write the next number in the sequence.

100,    55,    10,    _____

6   Use the number line to help you complete these number sentences.

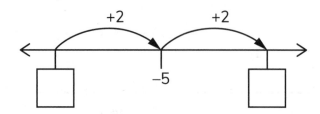

a   ☐ + 2 = –5              b   –5 + 2 = ☐

7   Here is part of a temperature scale showing the temperature
    at Coldpark.

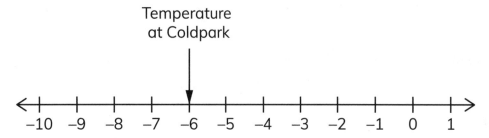

The temperature rises by 11 °C.

What is the new temperature?

_____

**Challenge**

8   The table shows the night-time temperatures on five days
    in Moscow.

| Day | Temperature °C |
|-----|----------------|
| Monday | –4 |
| Tuesday | –8 |
| Wednesday | 1 |
| Thursday | –9 |
| Friday | –6 |

a   The daytime temperature on Friday was 8 °C warmer than the temperature on Thursday night.

What was the daytime temperature on Friday?

_____

b   The night-time temperature on Saturday was 4 °C warmer than the temperature on Friday night.

What was the night-time temperature on Saturday?

_____

9   Classify the calculations by writing the letter of the calculation in the sorting diagram.

A   55 – 35          B   –35 – 515          C   10 – 47

D   –17 + 63          E   –218 + 8

|                   | addition calculation | subtraction calculation |
|-------------------|----------------------|-------------------------|
| positive answer   |                      |                         |
| negative answer   |                      |                         |

10  The table shows the temperature at 08:00 on three days.

| 1 January | 8 January | 15 January |
|-----------|-----------|------------|
| +1 °C     | –4 °C     | +3 °C      |

a   On 22 January the temperature is 7 °C lower than on 15 January.

What is the temperature on 22 January?   _____

b   Complete this calculation to show how much the temperature falls between 1 January and 8 January.

$1 - \boxed{\phantom{0}} = -4$

**11** Marcus writes a sequence of numbers.

His rule is to add 99 each time.

**a** Write the missing numbers in the sequence.

−500, ☐, ☐, ☐, ☐, ☐, ☐, ☐

Look at the ones digits of the numbers in the sequence.
What do you notice?

_____

_____

**b** Write a question about Marcus's sequence starting with
'What would happen if ...?'

Write an answer to your question.

_____

_____

_____

_____

_____

_____

# 6 3D shapes

## > 6.1 Nets of cubes and drawing 3D shapes

> cube
>
> open cube

**Worked example 1**

Which of these nets makes a cube?

A          B          C

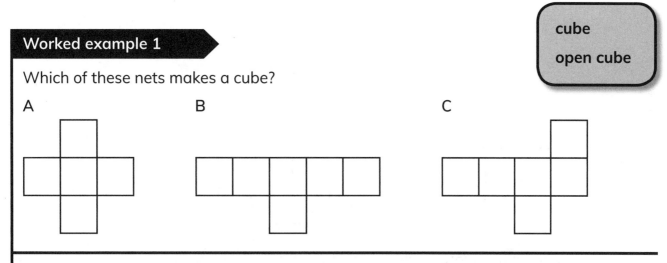

Net A does not have 6 square faces so A cannot be a net of a cube.

The faces on net B will overlap when it is folded so B cannot be the net of a cube.

Net C has 6 identical square faces that fold up without overlapping to give a cube.

**Answer:** Net C is the net of a cube.

Check if the net has 6 identical square faces.

Check if the 6 faces fold up along the edges so that none of them will overlap.

Check that the faces fold up along the edges and none of them overlap.

# Exercise 6.1

**Focus**

1 Draw a ring around the nets that make a cube.

A

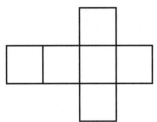

B

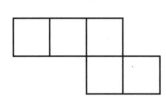

C

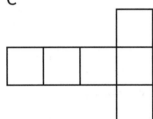

D

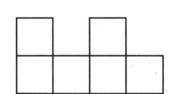

2 a Draw one more square on this net so that it will make an open cube.

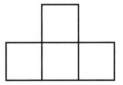

b Draw one more square on this net so that it will **not** make an open cube.

3   Draw lines to match the drawings to the models.
    The drawings are from a different angle.

A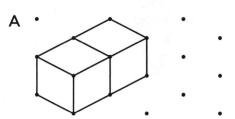

i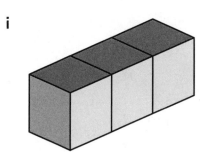

B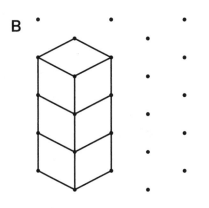

ii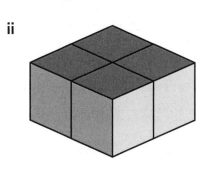

iii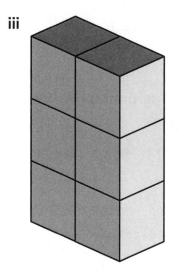

C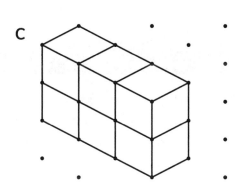

D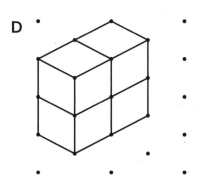

iv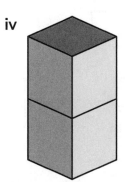

4 Name each shape and describe its properties.

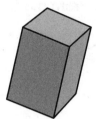

Shape A           Shape B           Shape C

a   Shape A is a _____ .

It has _____ faces, _____ edges and _____ vertices.

b   Shape B is a _____ .

It has _____ faces, _____ edges and _____ vertices.

c   Shape C is a _____ .

It has _____ faces, _____ edges and _____ vertices.

**Practice**

 5   Draw a cross (✗) through the nets that will **not** make a cube.

> **Tip**
>
> You could trace the nets onto paper then cut them out to check if they will fold to make a cube.

A

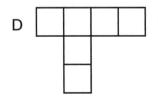

B

C

D

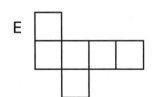

E

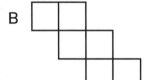

F

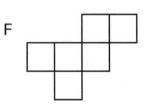

6  Use three colours. Colour two faces of this net in each colour.
   Colour the faces so that when the cube is made, opposite
   faces are the same colour.

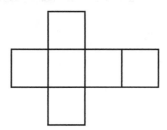

7  a  Draw this model made from cubes on the isometric paper.

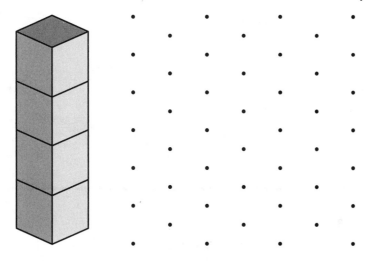

   b  Imagine the model was placed on its side.
      Draw the cubes in their new position.

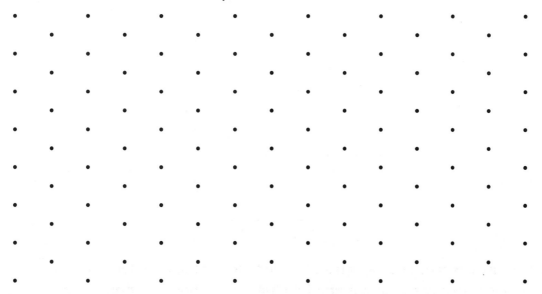

**Challenge**

  8   Use a pencil and ruler. Draw three different nets of a cube.

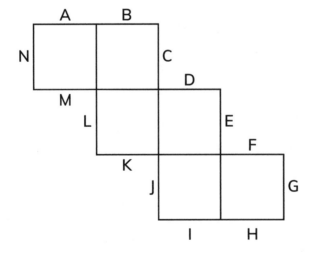

9   This shape is the net of a cube.
    The sides of the square faces are labelled with letters.

When the net is folded to make a cube, which sides will touch
along an edge?

When you have worked out which sides will touch along an edge,
trace the net onto paper. Cut out and fold the net to check your answers.

10 Visualise a square-based pyramid.

    a   Sketch the square-based pyramid from a direction where only one face can be seen.

    b   Sketch the square-based pyramid from a direction where only two faces can be seen.

    c   Sketch the square-based pyramid from a direction where exactly four faces can be seen.

# 7 ▶ Fractions, decimals and percentages

## › 7.1 Understanding fractions

**Worked example 1**

One tenth of a number is 5.

What is the number?

---

| denominator | operator |
|---|---|
| numerator | proper fraction |

---

$\frac{1}{10}$ of the number is 5.

The number ($\frac{10}{10}$) is

$5 \times 10 = 50$.

You can use a diagram to model the answer.

$\frac{1}{10}$

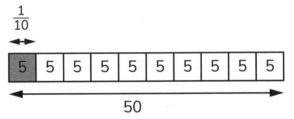

**Answer:** The number is 50.

## Exercise 7.1

**Focus**

1   Arun divides a cake into 4 equal pieces.

What fraction of the cake is each piece? _____

2   Show one way in which five children can share two pizzas
    equally between them.

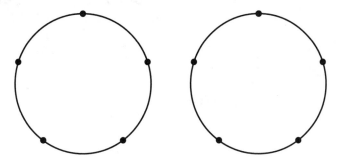

    How much pizza does each child get?

    _____

3   Calculate.

    a   $\frac{3}{4}$ of 36            b   $\frac{2}{3}$ of 24            c   $\frac{4}{5}$ of 25

    _____            _____            _____

**Practice**

4   This picture represents $\frac{1}{3}$ of a shape.

    It has 5 rectangles.

    Draw the whole shape.

    Can you find another way of doing it?

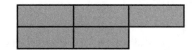

    How many rectangles are in the whole shape?

    _____

5  Calculate.

$\frac{1}{7}$ of 56        $\frac{2}{7}$ of 56        $\frac{3}{7}$ of 56        $\frac{2}{7}$ of 28        $\frac{4}{7}$ of 28

_____      _____      _____      _____      _____

What is the same about all the calculations?

What is the same about some of the calculations?

Explain your answer.

_____

_____

_____

6  Tick (✓) the statements that are true.

Put a cross (✗) next to and correct any statements that are false.

a  $\frac{3}{10}$ of 30 litres = 5 litres    ☐  _____

b  $\frac{4}{5}$ of 20 litres = 16 litres   ☐  _____

c  $\frac{5}{8}$ of 24 litres = 16 litres   ☐  _____

7  Draw a line from each calculation to the correct box.

$\frac{1}{2}$ of 40

$\frac{2}{5}$ of 60

$\frac{3}{4}$ of 16

$\frac{2}{3}$ of 30

Answer less than 20

Answer equal to 20

Answer more than 20

**Challenge**

8  One sixth of a number is 30.

What is the number?  _____

9 Zara says,

'To find $\frac{7}{10}$ of 100, I divide by 7 and multiply by 10.'

Explain what she has done wrong.

Correct her statement and find the correct answer.

_____

_____

10 Marcus has 42 stickers.

He gave $\frac{2}{7}$ of his stickers to Sofia and $\frac{1}{6}$ of his stickers to Arun.

How many stickers does Marcus have now?

_____

11 Zara, Sofia, Arun and Marcus show a method of answering the question:

If one-quarter of a number is 8, what is the number?

| Zara | Sofia |
|---|---|
| Multiply 8 by 4 | Divide 8 by 4 |
| **Arun** | **Marcus** |
| Double 8 and double the answer | 8 8 / 8 8 |

Which method would you use?

Which method would you not use?

Explain your answer.

_____

_____

## › 7.2 Percentages, decimals and fractions

**Worked example 2**

percentage

per cent

The table shows Amy's test results.

|  | Test result | Equivalent fraction | Percentage |
|---|---|---|---|
| **English** | $\frac{7}{10}$ | $\frac{\phantom{0}}{100}$ | |
| **Maths** | $\frac{9}{10}$ | $\frac{\phantom{0}}{100}$ | |
| **Science** | $\frac{8}{10}$ | $\frac{\phantom{0}}{100}$ | |

Complete the table to show her results.

**Answer:**

| Test result | Equivalent fraction | Percentage |
|---|---|---|
| $\frac{7}{10}$ | $\frac{70}{100}$ | 70% |
| $\frac{9}{10}$ | $\frac{90}{100}$ | 90% |
| $\frac{8}{10}$ | $\frac{80}{100}$ | 80% |

Change each fraction to an equivalent fraction with a denominator of 100, for example:

$$\frac{7}{10} = \frac{70}{100}$$ (×10)

Write the fraction as a percentage, remembering that a percentage is the number of parts out of a hundred.

# Exercise 7.2

**Focus**

1   Shade each scale to match the percentage.

   a   57%

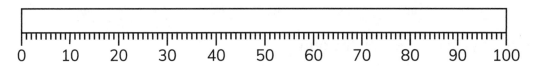

   b   81%

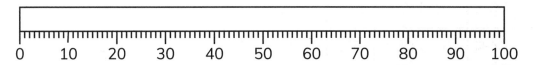

2   Write each fraction as a percentage.

   a   $\frac{9}{100}$ _____

   b   $\frac{1}{2}$ _____

   c   $\frac{1}{4}$ _____

   Shade the diagrams to represent the percentages.

   A 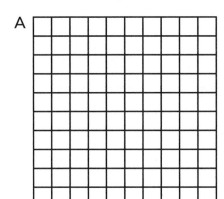   B 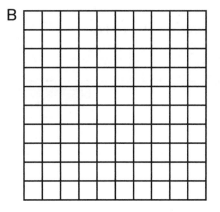   C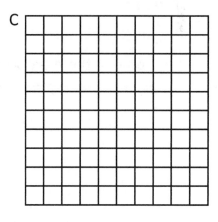

3   Find each fraction as a percentage.

$\dfrac{15}{100}$     $\dfrac{35}{100}$     $\dfrac{1}{2}$     $\dfrac{95}{100}$     $\dfrac{3}{4}$     $\dfrac{17}{100}$     $\dfrac{8}{100}$     $\dfrac{1}{4}$     $\dfrac{5}{100}$     $\dfrac{55}{100}$

____%  ____%  ____%  ____%  ____%  ____%  ____%  ____%  ____%  ____%

Shade each of your answers on the grid.

| 1%  | 99% | 35% | 75%  | 8%  |
|-----|-----|-----|------|-----|
| 40% | 70% | 25% | 100% | 17% |
| 12% | 44% | 15% | 95%  | 5%  |
| 20% | 38% | 50% | 34%  | 30% |
| 90% | 60% | 55% | 65%  | 4%  |

What letter is revealed?        _____

**Practice**

4   Marcus represents 9% in different ways.

Some of them are wrong.

| 0.09 | <br><br> | $\dfrac{9}{10}$ |
|------|----------|-----------------|
|      | 9 hundredths | 0.9 |
|      | $\dfrac{9}{100}$ | 9 tenths |

Put a cross (✗) through any answers that are incorrect.

Explain what Marcus has done wrong.

_____

_____

5   Draw lines to join each fraction to the equivalent decimal.

$\frac{7}{10}$

$\frac{1}{2}$

$\frac{3}{10}$

0.2

0.3

0.4

0.5

0.6

0.7

6   This diagram contains an equivalent fraction, decimal and percentage.

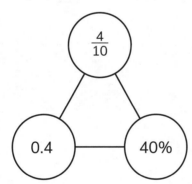

Complete these diagrams.

a

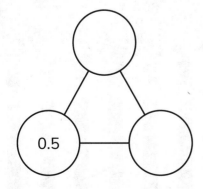

b

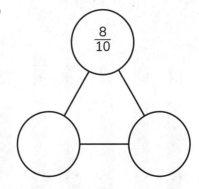

## Challenge

7 This fence has ten sections of equal length.

Omar paints three sections of the fence.

    a   What percentage of the fence does Omar paint? _____

    b   What fraction of the fence is not painted? _____

8 Here is a grid of ten squares.

    a   What fraction of the grid is shaded? _____

    b   Write this fraction as a decimal and as a percentage.

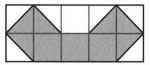

_____

9   Look at this set of fractions and percentages.

$$\frac{75}{100} \qquad \frac{3}{10} \qquad \frac{10}{100} \qquad \frac{15}{150} \qquad \frac{50}{200} \qquad \frac{1}{10} \qquad \frac{1}{2}$$

$$\frac{25}{100} \qquad \frac{3}{4} \qquad \frac{1}{4} \qquad \frac{30}{40} \qquad \frac{60}{120} \qquad \frac{50}{100}$$

10%      75%      25%      50%

a   Write down four sets of equivalent fractions and percentages.
Each set has three equivalent fractions and one percentage.

_____

_____

_____

_____

b   Complete the table for the fraction you did not use.

| Fraction | Equivalent fractions | | Percentage |
|---|---|---|---|
|  |  |  |  |

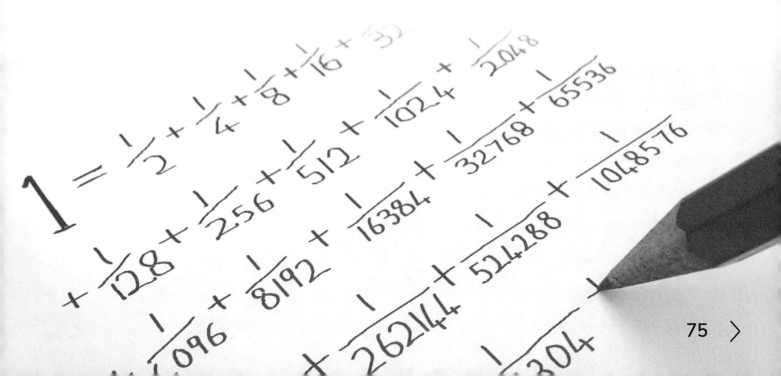

# > 7.3 Equivalence and comparison

**Worked example 3**

Join each improper fraction to the correct place on the number line.

improper fraction

mixed number

$$\frac{5}{4} \qquad \frac{3}{2} \qquad \frac{11}{8}$$

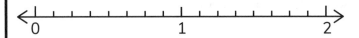

$\frac{5}{4} = 1\frac{1}{4} = 1\frac{2}{8}$

$\frac{3}{2} = 1\frac{1}{2} = 1\frac{4}{8}$

$\frac{11}{8} = 1\frac{3}{8}$

It is easier to mark on the fractions if you write them as mixed numbers.

The line is divided into eighths so write the fraction part of the mixed numbers in eighths.

**Answer:**

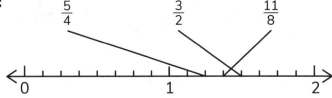

## Exercise 7.3

**Focus**

1   Write these fractions and decimals in order starting with the smallest.

a   3.4,  5.3,  3.5,  1.9,  2.7

b   $\frac{3}{7}$,     $\frac{6}{7}$,     $\frac{1}{7}$,     $\frac{4}{7}$,     $\frac{2}{7}$

2   Write what these diagrams show as a mixed number and
    an improper fraction.

Example:  $\boxed{\frac{1}{4}}\boxed{\frac{1}{4}}\boxed{\frac{1}{4}}\boxed{\frac{1}{4}}$   $\boxed{\frac{1}{4}}\boxed{\frac{1}{4}}\boxed{\frac{1}{4}}$   $\frac{7}{4} = 1\frac{3}{4}$

a

$\frac{1}{4}$  $\frac{1}{4}$  $\frac{1}{4}$  $\frac{1}{4}$   |   $\frac{1}{4}$  $\frac{1}{4}$

$\frac{1}{4}$  $\frac{1}{4}$  $\frac{1}{4}$  $\frac{1}{4}$

_____

b   $\boxed{\frac{1}{5}}\boxed{\frac{1}{5}}\boxed{\frac{1}{5}}\boxed{\frac{1}{5}}\boxed{\frac{1}{5}}$   $\boxed{\frac{1}{5}}\boxed{\frac{1}{5}}\boxed{\frac{1}{5}}$

$\boxed{\frac{1}{5}}\boxed{\frac{1}{5}}\boxed{\frac{1}{5}}\boxed{\frac{1}{5}}\boxed{\frac{1}{5}}$

$\boxed{\frac{1}{5}}\boxed{\frac{1}{5}}\boxed{\frac{1}{5}}\boxed{\frac{1}{5}}\boxed{\frac{1}{5}}$

_____

3   Write the missing numbers.

$0.5 = \dfrac{\boxed{\phantom{0}}}{10} = \dfrac{1}{\boxed{\phantom{0}}}$

Now use one of the symbols < or > to complete these statements.

$\dfrac{4}{10}$ $\boxed{\phantom{0}}$ $0.5$        $0.6$ $\boxed{\phantom{0}}$ $\dfrac{1}{2}$

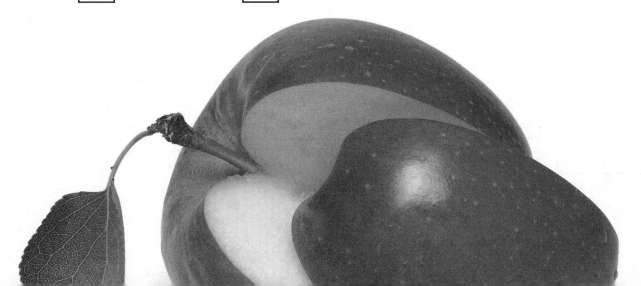

4   Use these number lines to help you complete the table of
    equivalent fractions, decimals and percentages.

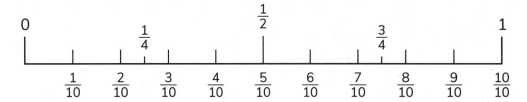

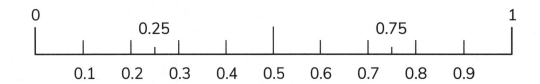

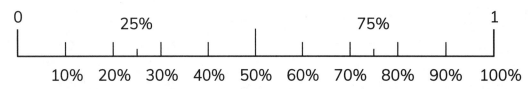

| Fraction | Decimal | Percentage |
|----------|---------|------------|
| $\frac{1}{10}$ | | |
| | 0.6 | |
| $\frac{3}{10}$ | | |
| | | 75% |
| $\frac{5}{10}$ | | |
| | 0.2 | |
| | | 40% |

| Fraction | Decimal | Percentage |
|----------|---------|------------|
| $\frac{10}{10}$ | 1 | |
| $\frac{1}{4}$ | | |
| | 0.8 | |
| $\frac{1}{2}$ | | |
| $\frac{9}{10}$ | | |
| | | 70% |

## Practice

5   Here are three improper fractions.

Join each one to the correct position on the number line.

$$\frac{7}{4} \qquad \frac{5}{2} \qquad \frac{6}{3}$$

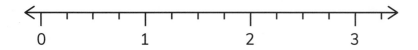

6   Change these improper fractions into mixed numbers.

a   $\frac{5}{4}$          b   $\frac{9}{5}$          c   $\frac{10}{3}$

_____          _____          _____

d   $\frac{6}{4}$          e   $\frac{7}{3}$          f   $\frac{9}{6}$

_____          _____          _____

7   Draw a ring around all the numbers that are equivalent to $\frac{1}{4}$.

$$\frac{25}{100} \qquad 50\% \qquad \frac{2}{5} \qquad 0.75 \qquad 0.25$$

8   Use one of the symbols <, > or = to complete each statement.

a   $\frac{2}{5}$ ☐ 50%          b   60% ☐ $\frac{3}{5}$          c   25% ☐ $\frac{1}{5}$

## Challenge

9   Igor says, '25% is smaller than $\frac{2}{5}$.'

Explain why Igor is correct.

_____

_____

**10** Join pairs of equivalent fractions and decimals.

$3\frac{1}{4}$

$1\frac{4}{5}$

$\frac{16}{10}$

3.25

2.75

$2\frac{3}{4}$

$2\frac{2}{5}$

2.4

$2\frac{7}{10}$

$\frac{7}{2}$

2.7

1.6

3.5

1.8

**11** Write these fractions, decimals and percentages in order starting with the smallest.

a   $\frac{3}{4}$     0.7     $\frac{1}{2}$     0.2     30%

_____

b   0.3     $\frac{3}{5}$     45%     $\frac{1}{5}$     0.5

_____

# 8 ▶ Probability

## › 8.1 Likelihood

**Worked example 1**

Describe the likelihood of these outcomes.

A  Taking a white ball out of this bag.

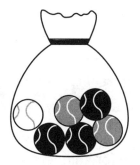

B  Rolling an even number on a 6-sided dice.

Which outcome is more likely?

| certain | likely |
| equally likely | outcome |
| even chance | unlikely |
| impossible | |

---

A  There are 6 balls.

1 ball is white.

Most of the balls are not white.

Taking a white ball is unlikely.

> Work out how likely you are to take a white ball out of the bag.

B  There are 6 possible outcomes when the dice is rolled.

3 of the outcomes are even numbers.

3 of the outcomes are not even numbers.

There is the same chance of rolling an even number as not rolling an even number.

There is an even chance of rolling an even number.

> Work out how likely you are to roll an even number on a 6-sided dice.

**Answer:** Rolling an even number on a 6-sided dice is more likely than taking a white ball out of the bag.

# Exercise 8.1

**Focus**

1   Label the likelihood scale with these words.

likely     certain     impossible     even chance     unlikely

2   Arun has a bag with only red apples in it.

Complete the sentences.

The likelihood of Arun taking a red apple is _____ .

The likelihood of Arun taking a green apple is _____ .

> **Tip**
>
> In question 3, look for spinners where the chance of spinning a 1 is the same as the chance of spinning a 2.

3   Draw a ring around the spinners where you are equally likely to spin a 1 or a 2.

A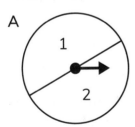

B

C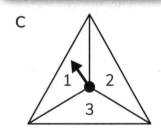

D

E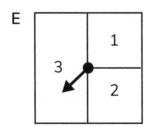

F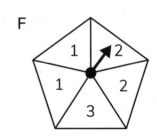

**Practice**

4   Draw a likelihood scale using the words 'impossible', 'unlikely', 'even chance', 'likely' and 'certain'. Label it with arrows to show the likelihood of each outcome A to F when you spin this spinner.

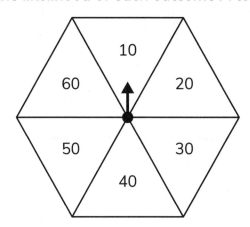

A   A multiple of 10.

B   A number greater than 35.

C   An even number.

D   A number less than 5.

E   A number between 15 and 100.

F   A multiple of 3.

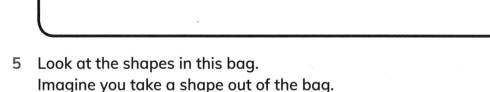

5   Look at the shapes in this bag.
Imagine you take a shape out of the bag.

Draw a ring around **True** or **False** for each statement.

a   It is likely that the shape is a triangle.           True / False

b   It is impossible that the shape will be a pentagon.   True / False

c   There is an even chance of taking a square.          True / False

d   Taking a hexagon or a circle is equally likely.      True / False

e   Taking a square is more likely than taking a triangle.   True / False

6 Play this game 10 times.

Put 3 black counters and 2 white counters into a bag.

Pull a counter out of the bag without looking.

If the counter is black move one place to the right.

If the counter is white move one place to the left.

Put the counter back into the bag.

Take counters until you reach 'WIN' or 'LOSE'.

| LOSE | | | | Start | | | | WIN |

Record your results in the table.

|  | Tally | Frequency |
|---|---|---|
| **Win** | | |
| **Lose** | | |

 Do you think that winning and losing are equally likely? Why?

_____

_____

**Challenge**

7 Use this space to design and colour or label a spinner that matches these statements.

- It is not equally likely that the spinner will land on green or blue.

- It is not impossible for the spinner to land on orange.

- There is an even chance of spinning red.

- It is equally likely that the spinner will land on yellow or brown.

- It is unlikely that the spinner will land on pink.

8 Marcus says that the likelihood of this spinner landing on 1 is an even chance because all the numbers are equally likely.
Marcus has made a mistake.

What is wrong with Marcus's statement?
Explain your answer.

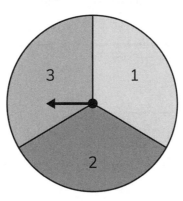

_____

_____

_____

# > 8.2 Experiments and simulations

### Worked example 2

Carry out an experiment to investigate the likelihood of rolling a six on a six-sided dice.

simulation

| | |
|---|---|
| I think that rolling a six is unlikely. | Write a prediction of what might happen. |

| Outcome | Tally | Frequency |
|---------|-------|-----------|
| Not six | ⊞⊞ ⊞⊞ ⊞⊞ ⊞⊞ ⊞ I | 26 |
| Six | IIII | 4 |

Draw a table to collect the data.

Roll the dice many times and record the outcomes in the table.

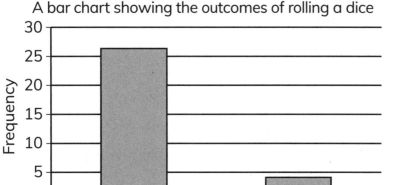

A bar chart showing the outcomes of rolling a dice

You could display the data in a graph.

The result suggests that rolling a six is unlikely, which is what I predicted. I should roll the dice more times to check.

Compare the result to your prediction.

**Answer:** Rolling a 6 is unlikely.

# Exercise 8.2

**Focus**

1 You are going to flip a coin 100 times and record if it lands on heads or tails.

 a Predict your results.

 I think that _____

 _____

 b Flip the coin 100 times and record the results in the table.

| Outcome | Tally | Frequency |
|---------|-------|-----------|
| Heads | | |
| Tails | | |
| | **Total** | 100 |

 c Complete the bar chart with your results.

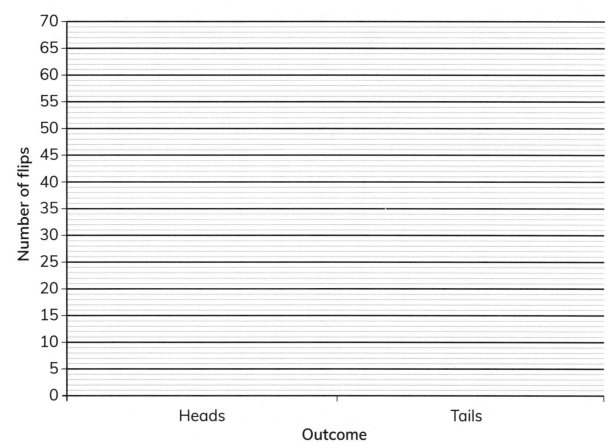

   **d**   Do your results agree with your prediction?

_____

   **e**   Write a sentence about what you have found out.

_____

 **2**   Mia has a bag of letter tiles.

   She takes one tile out of the bag at a time.
   She writes the letter, then puts the tile back into the bag.

   These are the letters she takes.

       D    A    B    A    A    A    B    D    B

   Draw a ring around the bags that Mia could be using.

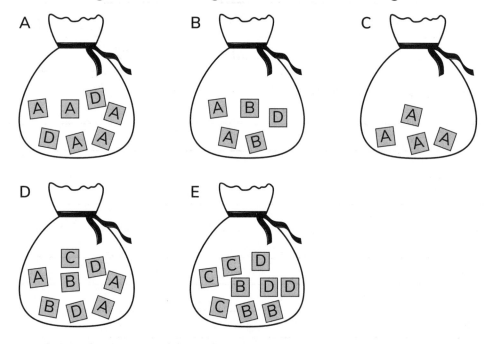

   Explain why Mia could not be using bag E.

_____

_____

### Practice

3   Marcus says, 'There is an even chance of flipping a head. My first flip was a head so my next flip must be a tail.'

Is Marcus correct? Explain your answer.

_____

_____

4   Draw symbols on each of these 8 cards so that:

- there is an even chance of choosing a card with a square on it

- taking a card with a triangle or a card with a circle are equally likely.

Make your set of 8 cards using card or paper.

Take and replace a card 30 times and record the outcomes in the box.

Write two sentences about the outcomes of your experiment.

_____

_____

**Challenge**

5   A bag contains 5 coloured balls.

Hari takes a ball from the bag. He writes down the colour then replaces the ball into the bag.

These are the colours of the balls he took from the bag.

Red, red, yellow, yellow, yellow, red, green, red, red, green, yellow, red.

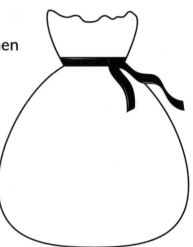

a   Draw coloured balls in the bag to show what you predict is in Hari's bag.

b   Explain your prediction.

_____

_____

_____

_____

6   Here is a treasure chest full of coins.

There are bronze, silver and gold coins.

Each type of coin is equally likely to be taken from the chest.
Imagine taking one coin at a time from the chest.

Design a spinner to simulate which type of coin is taken from
the treasure chest.

Using a pencil and a paper clip, spin your spinner 30 times
to simulate taking 30 coins from the treasure chest.

Record your results.

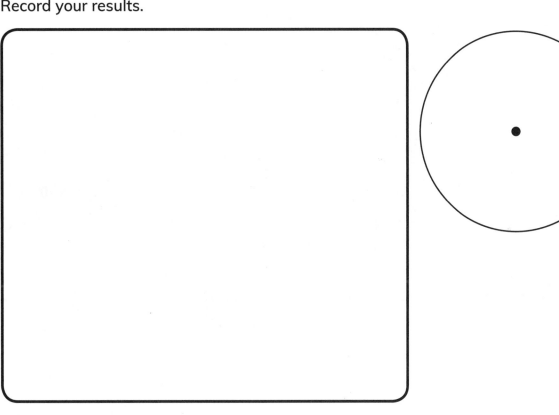

Look at the results of your simulation.

a   How many bronze coins did you take?   _____

b   How many silver coins did you take?   _____

c   How many gold coins did you take?   _____

d In your simulation did you take an equal
   number of bronze, silver and gold coins? _____

e Would you expect to take an equal number of bronze,
   silver and gold coins? Explain your answer.

_____

_____

_____

# 9 ▶ Addition and subtraction of fractions

## > 9.1 Addition and subtraction of fractions

### Worked example 1

Use a diagram to help you calculate $\dfrac{2}{3} - \dfrac{5}{12}$.

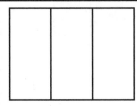

12 is a multiple of 3.

Draw a diagram divided into thirds.

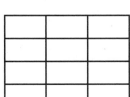

Add extra lines to divide the diagram into twelfths.

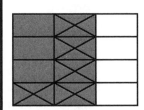

Shade $\dfrac{2}{3}$ $(= \dfrac{8}{12})$.

Then cross out $\dfrac{5}{12}$.

$\dfrac{3}{12}$ remains shaded.

**Answer:**

$\dfrac{2}{3} - \dfrac{5}{12} = \dfrac{3}{12}$

# Exercise 9.1

**Focus**

1   Use the fraction wall to help you with the calculations.

a   $\dfrac{1}{2} + \dfrac{3}{8} = \boxed{\phantom{0}}$          b   $\dfrac{3}{4} - \dfrac{1}{8} = \boxed{\phantom{0}}$          c   $\dfrac{3}{4} + \dfrac{2}{8} = \boxed{\phantom{0}}$

| 1 | | | | | | | |
|---|---|---|---|---|---|---|---|
| $\frac{1}{2}$ | | | | $\frac{1}{2}$ | | | |
| $\frac{1}{4}$ | | $\frac{1}{4}$ | | $\frac{1}{4}$ | | $\frac{1}{4}$ | |
| $\frac{1}{8}$ | $\frac{1}{8}$ | $\frac{1}{8}$ | $\frac{1}{8}$ | $\frac{1}{8}$ | $\frac{1}{8}$ | $\frac{1}{8}$ | $\frac{1}{8}$ |

2   Use the fraction wall to help you with the calculations.

a   $\dfrac{5}{6} - \dfrac{1}{12} = \boxed{\phantom{0}}$          b   $\dfrac{2}{3} + \dfrac{1}{6} = \boxed{\phantom{0}}$          c   $\dfrac{7}{12} - \dfrac{1}{3} = \boxed{\phantom{0}}$

| 1 | | | | | | | | | | | |
|---|---|---|---|---|---|---|---|---|---|---|---|
| $\frac{1}{3}$ | | | | $\frac{1}{3}$ | | | | $\frac{1}{3}$ | | | |
| $\frac{1}{6}$ | | $\frac{1}{6}$ | | $\frac{1}{6}$ | | $\frac{1}{6}$ | | $\frac{1}{6}$ | | $\frac{1}{6}$ | |
| $\frac{1}{12}$ | $\frac{1}{12}$ | $\frac{1}{12}$ | $\frac{1}{12}$ | $\frac{1}{12}$ | $\frac{1}{12}$ | $\frac{1}{12}$ | $\frac{1}{12}$ | $\frac{1}{12}$ | $\frac{1}{12}$ | $\frac{1}{12}$ | $\frac{1}{12}$ |

3   Use the diagrams to help you with the calculations.

a   $\dfrac{5}{6} + \dfrac{7}{12} = \boxed{\phantom{0}}$          b   $\dfrac{11}{12} - \dfrac{5}{6} = \boxed{\phantom{0}}$

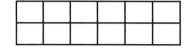

4  Use the number line to help you with the calculations.

a  $\dfrac{5}{8} + \dfrac{1}{4} =$ ☐

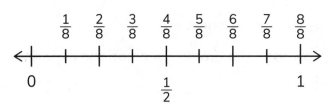

b  $\dfrac{7}{8} - \dfrac{3}{4} =$ ☐

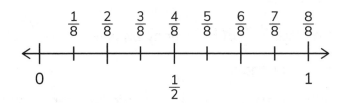

## Practice

You can draw diagrams to help you answer these questions.

5  Calculate.

a  $\dfrac{2}{5} + \dfrac{2}{15} =$ ☐

b  $\dfrac{11}{12} + \dfrac{5}{6} =$ ☐

c  $\dfrac{7}{12} + \dfrac{3}{4} =$ ☐

6  Calculate.

a  $\dfrac{5}{6} - \dfrac{2}{3} =$ ☐

b  $\dfrac{9}{20} - \dfrac{1}{5} =$ ☐

c  $\dfrac{11}{12} - \dfrac{1}{4} =$ ☐

7   Emma spent $\frac{3}{4}$ hour preparing an experiment and $\frac{5}{8}$ hour doing the experiment.

How long did Emma spend on the experiment altogether?

_____

8   Ravi spent $\frac{1}{5}$ of his money on a bag and $\frac{7}{10}$ of his money on a pair of shoes.

What fraction of his money did he spend altogether?

_____

9   The shaded parts of the fraction strips represent two fractions.

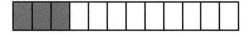

a   What is the sum of the two fractions? Write the calculation and the answer. Show all your working.

_____

b   What is the difference between the two fractions? Write the calculation and the answer. Show all your working.

_____

**Challenge**

10  Arun painted a rectangle in green, red and blue.

He painted $\frac{5}{8}$ green and $\frac{1}{4}$ red.

What fraction did he paint blue?

_____

11 Calculate $1 - \dfrac{1}{4} - \dfrac{3}{8}$

_____

 12 Which subtraction is the odd one out?

A $\dfrac{13}{4} - \dfrac{3}{8}$ B $\dfrac{1}{3} - \dfrac{2}{9}$ C $\dfrac{23}{7} - \dfrac{8}{7}$

Explain your answer.

_____

_____

13 Write the missing numbers.

a $\dfrac{\Box}{12} + \dfrac{3}{4} = \dfrac{14}{12}$ b $\dfrac{3}{5} - \dfrac{\Box}{10} = \dfrac{1}{10}$

14 Ravi's class voted for where to go on their class outing.

$\dfrac{3}{4}$ of the class voted for the theme park.

$\dfrac{1}{8}$ of the class voted for the museum.

The rest of the class voted for a river trip.

What fraction of the class voted for the river trip?

_____

# 10 ▶ Angles

## › 10.1 Angles

---

**Worked example 1**

What is the missing angle on this straight line?

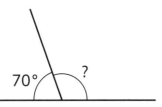

70°  ?

The angles on a straight line add up to 180°.

Either:

70° + ? = 180°

70° + **110**° = 180°

Or

180° − 70° = ?

180° − 70° = **110**°

**Answer:** The missing angle is 110°.

Work out what you need to add to 70 to equal 180.

Or subtract 70 from 180 to work out the missing angle.

---

> angle
>
> degrees (°)
>
> reflex angle

---

## Exercise 10.1

**Focus**

1   Draw a ring around the reflex angles.

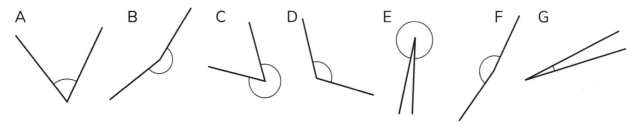

A          B          C          D          E          F   G

**2** Draw a ring around the closest estimate for each angle.

a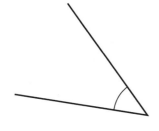

b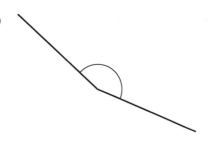

c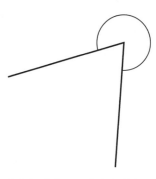

40° 90° 140° 240°  60° 160° 180° 260°  20° 90° 190° 290°

**3** The angles on a straight line add up to 180°.

Work out the missing angle on each of these straight lines.

a  170° + ? = 180°

The missing angle is _____ .

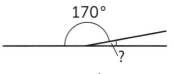

b  100° + ? = 180°

The missing angle is _____ .

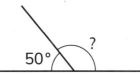

c  50° + ? = 180°

The missing angle is _____ .

> **Tip**
>
> Remember to use ° for degrees.

**Practice**

4   Draw a ring around the greater of each pair of angles.

a   A           B

b   A 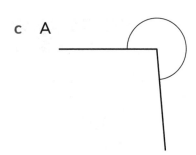          B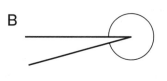

c   A 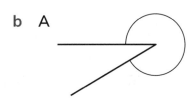          B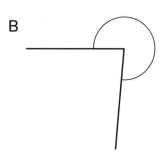

 5   Label the angles inside the vertices of this shape 'acute', 'obtuse', 'reflex' or 'right angle'.

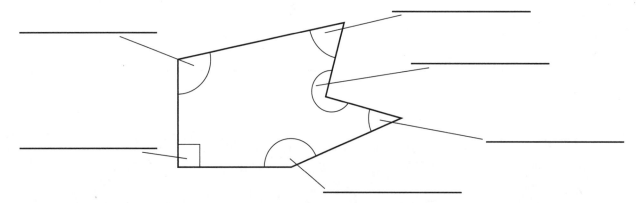

 6   Complete the sentences.

_____ angles are less than 360 ° and greater than 180 °.

Acute angles are _____ than _____ .

_____ angles are _____ than _____ and greater than 90 °.

7   Part of each rainbow is missing.
    What is the angle of the missing part?

a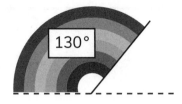

130°

_____

b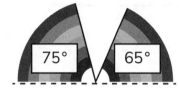

75°    65°

_____

c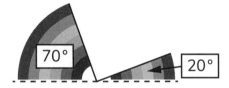

70°    20°

_____

d

35°    45°

_____

## Challenge

8   The angles X and Y are the same size. Work out the angles.
    Record your working clearly or explain how you worked out your answer.

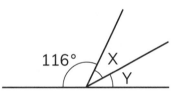

116°   X
        Y

X = _____         Y = _____

_____

9   Half of this cake remains and it is going to be cut into three
    pieces from the centre of the original cake to the edge.
    At what angle should the pieces be cut so that all
    three pieces are the same size?

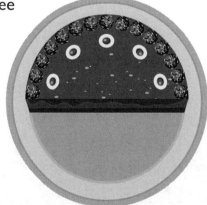

_____

10 Make a poster here of everything you know about angles.
Include lots of angle vocabulary.

# and division

> ## 11.1 Multiplication

**Worked example 1**

Write the missing digits to make the calculation correct.

$$
\begin{array}{r}
\boxed{\phantom{0}}\ 7\ \boxed{\phantom{0}} \\
\times\ \ \ \ 6 \\
\hline
1\quad 0\quad 6\quad 2
\end{array}
$$

product

$$
\begin{array}{r}
\boxed{\phantom{0}}\ 7\ \boxed{2} \\
\times\quad 6 \\
\hline
3\quad 2 \\
\hline
4\quad 1
\end{array}
$$

Think about what numbers can go in the ones box.

To give 2 in the ones place in the answer, the 6 must be multiplied by either 2 or 7.

Try 2 and continue the multiplication. The 3 in the tens column is incorrect so 2 cannot be right.

$$
\begin{array}{r}
\boxed{\phantom{0}}\ 7\ \boxed{7} \\
\times\quad 6 \\
\hline
1\quad 0\quad 6\quad 2 \\
\hline
4\quad 4
\end{array}
$$

Try 7 and continue the multiplication.

$$
\begin{array}{r}
\boxed{1}\ 7\ \boxed{7} \\
\times\quad 6 \\
\hline
1\quad 0\quad 6\quad 2 \\
\hline
4\quad 4
\end{array}
$$

The calculation can be completed by writing 1 in the hundreds box.

When you try different numbers to find the ones that work, you are **specialising**.

# Exercise 11.1

**Focus**

**Tip**

Remember to estimate before you calculate.

1   Ravi travels 224 km a week in his car.

    How far does he travel in 8 weeks?

    _____

2   The top number in each pattern is the product of the two numbers below it.

    Complete this pattern.

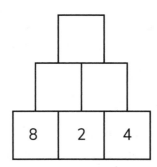

 3   Write the missing digits to make the calculation correct. Remember to estimate before you calculate.

$$
\begin{array}{r}
\boxed{\phantom{0}}\ 5\ \boxed{\phantom{0}} \\
\times\quad\ 7 \\
\hline
1\quad 0\quad 6\quad 4
\end{array}
$$

4   Fatima's heart beats about 79 times each minute.

    About how many times does her heart beat in an hour? _____

**Practice**

5   A small theatre has 22 rows of 18 seats.

    How many seats are there altogether? _____

6   Calculate.

    a   54 × 87                        b   98 × 36




    _____                          _____

7   Calculate 13 × 13 and 31 × 31.

    What do you notice about the results?

    _____

8   Sofia multiplied 76 by 68.

    Here is her working.

    |   |   | 7 | 6 |
    |---|---|---|---|
    | × |   | 6 | 8 |
    | 4 | 2 | 6 | 0 |
    |   | 5 | 6 | 8 |
    | 4 | 8 | 2 | 8 |
    |   | 1 |   |   |

    What errors has Sofia made? How should she improve her work?

    Calculate the correct answer.

    _____

    _____

**Challenge**

9  Here are four digit cards.

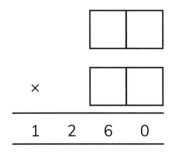

Use these cards to complete the calculation.

```
     ☐☐
  ×   ☐☐
  ─────────
   1  2  6  0
  ─────────
```

10 Calculate.

a  268 × 57                    b  386 × 79

_____                    _____

11 The top number in each shape is the product of the two numbers below it.

Complete these shapes.

a

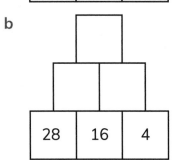

| 7 | 17 | 4 |

b

| 28 | 16 | 4 |

12 Here are four digit cards.

| 0 | 2 | 5 | 7 |

Use these cards to complete the calculation.

Each card can only be used once.

☐☐ × ☐☐ = 1500

13 Twenty-five lamp posts are equally spaced along a road.

**Tip**

Think about how many spaces there are between the lamp posts.

The posts are 180 metres apart.

What is the distance between the first and last lamp post in kilometres? _____

# > 11.2 Division

| Worked example 2 | decompose |  inverse operations |
| --- | --- | --- |

**Worked example 2**

Calculate $95 \div 8$.

Write the remainder as a fraction.

decompose       inverse operations

denominator       numerator

divisor

Estimate: $80 \div 8 = 10$.

So the answer will be a little greater than 10.

|   | 1 | 1 | r7 |
| --- | --- | --- | --- |
| 8 | 9 | $^1$5 |   |

**Answer:** $95 \div 8 = 11\dfrac{7}{8}$

Make an estimate then complete the division to find the remainder.

The remainder of 7 is the numerator of the fraction.

The divisor of 8 is the denominator of the fraction.

## Exercise 11.2

**Focus**

1   Here is a number square.

| 101 | 102 | 103 | 104 | 105 |
| --- | --- | --- | --- | --- |
| 106 | 107 | 108 | 109 | 110 |
| 111 | 112 | 113 | 114 | 115 |
| 116 | 117 | 118 | 119 | 120 |
| 121 | 122 | 123 | 124 | 125 |

Each number is divided by 9.

Draw a ring around all the numbers that have a remainder of 4.

2   A number line goes from 0 to 200 in five equal steps.

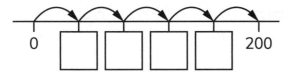

Write the missing numbers on the number line.

3   Divide 216 by 8. Remember to estimate before you calculate.

_____

4   Write these calculations in the correct part of the table.

| 120 ÷ 8 | 84 ÷ 6 | 105 ÷ 5 | 81 ÷ 9 |

| Less than 10 | Between 10 and 20 | More than 20 |
|---|---|---|
|  |  |  |

5   Sofia writes 136 ÷ 5 = 27 remainder 1.

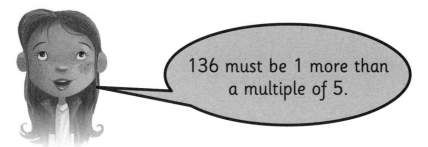

136 must be 1 more than a multiple of 5.

Is Sofia correct? How do you know?

_____

_____

## Practice

6  Zara says, 'The answer to 93 divided by 4 can be written as

23 remainder 1 or $23\frac{1}{4}$.

Do you agree?

Explain your answer.

7  Calculate, writing the remainder as a fraction.

   a  $92 \div 5$          b  $91 \div 4$          c  $97 \div 7$

   _____          _____          _____

8  Calculate writing the remainder as a fraction.

   a  $317 \div 5$          b  $567 \div 8$          c  $943 \div 6$

   _____          _____          _____

## Challenge

9  Write the missing digit.

   | | 0 | 6 | $\div$ | 9 | $= 45\frac{1}{9}$

10 Write the missing digit.

   | 1 | 0 | | $\div$ | 4 | $= 26\frac{1}{4}$

11 A school secretary needs to order 185 exercise books.

   The exercise books are sold in packs of 8.

   How many complete packs of exercise books should he order?

   _____

# 〉 11.3 Tests of divisibility

| Worked example 3 | | divisible |
|---|---|---|
| | | divisibility test |
| | | Venn diagram |

Use divisibility tests to work out whether these numbers are divisible by 4.

134    204    3154    42 124    45 244    6214

How did you work out your answer?

| | |
|---|---|
| 34 – not divisible by 4 | Look at the last two digits (tens and ones) of each number. If that number is a multiple of 4, the whole number is divisible by 4. |
| 4 – divisible by 4 | |
| 54 – not divisible by 4 | |
| 24 – divisible by 4 | If the ones digit is 4, the tens digit must be even. So, 4, 24 and 44 are divisible by 4 but |
| 44 – divisible by 4 | |
| 14 – not divisible by 4 | 34, 54 and 14 are not divisible by 4. |

**Answer:** 204, 42 124, 45 244 are divisible by 4.

## Exercise 11.3

**Focus**

1   Draw a ring around the numbers that are divisible by 4.

   96      154      1044      132      522

2   What is the smallest number that can be added to 333 to make it **exactly** divisible by 4?

   _____

3   Write these numbers in the Venn diagram.

400        604        28        36        116        101        64

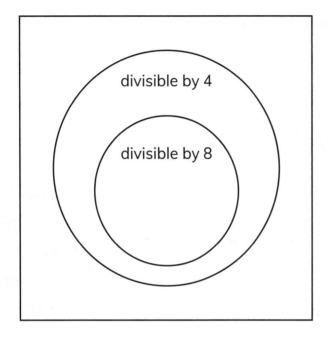

 4   Here are four labels.

( odd )   ( divisible by 8 )   ( not divisible by 8 )   ( not odd )

Write each label in the correct place on the sorting diagram.

|  |  |  |
|---|---|---|
|  |  | 37        101 |
|  | 48        96 | 54        78 |

**Practice**

5   Sofia says, 'All numbers that end in 4 are divisible by 4.'

Is Sofia correct? How do you know?

_____

_____

6   Complete this number so that it is divisible by 4.

| 5 | 9 | 3 | 1 | 3 |   |

7   Look at this set of numbers.

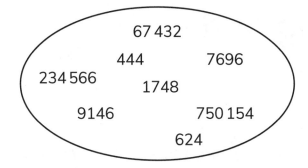

67 432
444          7696
234 566
1748
9146                  750 154
624

a   Write the numbers that are divisible by 4.

_____

b   Write the numbers that are divisible by 8.

_____

**Challenge**

 8   Arun is thinking of a multiple of 3 that is less than 50.

He says, 'My number is divisible by 8.'

Which numbers could Arun be thinking of?

_____

 9   Complete this number so that it is divisible by 8.

| 5 | 8 | 2 | 1 | 7 |   |

 10  Here are four digit cards.

| 5 |   | 7 |   | 3 |   | 2 |

Use each card once to make a total that is divisible by 8

| | |  +  | | |

# 12 Data

## > 12.1 Representing and interpreting data

Worked example 1

Use this dot plot to find out how many of the children scored more than 6 marks in the test.

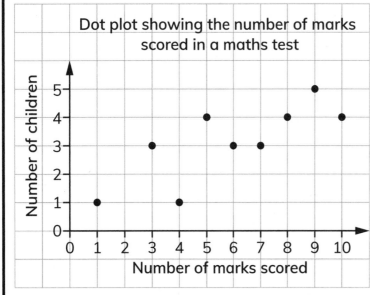

bar chart    statistical question

data    waffle diagram

dot plot

**Continued**

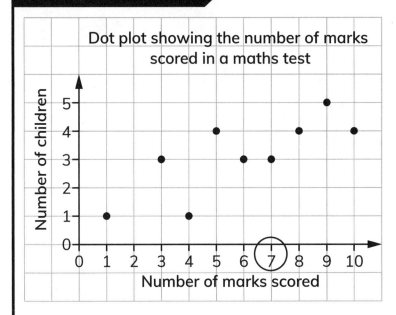

Find the first category that is more than 6.

7 is greater than 6.

Remember that 6 is not more than 6.

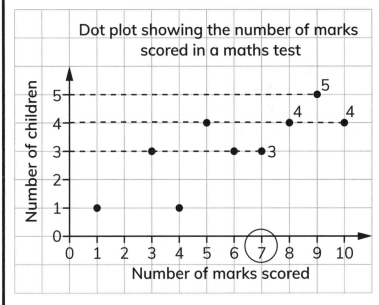

Use the scale on the y-axis to find out what each dot represents and how many children there are in each category that is more than 6.

3 + 4 + 5 + 4 = 16

Find the total of all the children in the categories more than 6.

**Answer:** 16 children scored more than 6 marks.

# Exercise 12.1

**Focus**

1   Look at this dot plot.

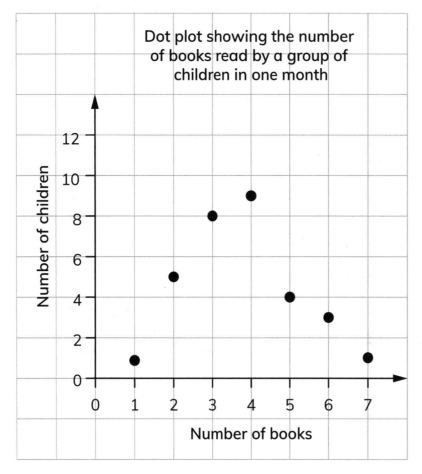

a   How many children have read 2 books?

_____

b   How many children have read more than 4 books?

_____

c   Harry says that 14 children read fewer than 3 books.
Is that true or false?

_____

2   This table shows the favourite flavours of ice cream of some
    people in a café.

| Flavour | Tally | Total |
|---------|-------|-------|
| Strawberry | HHI III | |
| Chocolate | HHI HHI I | |
| Vanilla | III | |
| Mint | HHI II | |

a   Complete the totals in the table.

b   Use the table to complete the bar chart.

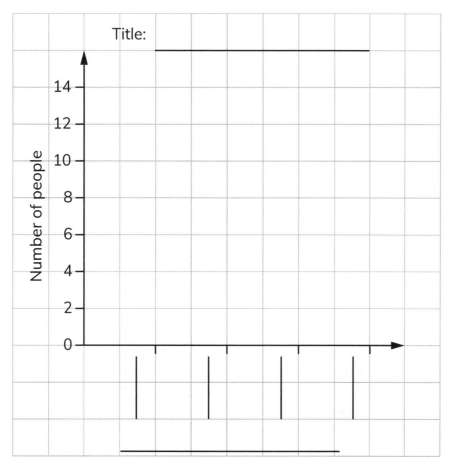

3   This table shows the birds Jo saw in a garden one day.

| Bird | Sparrow | Robin | Pigeon | Crow |
|------|---------|-------|--------|------|
| Frequency | 10 | 5 | 2 | 3 |

a   Draw a ring around the grid which is best to use for a
     waffle diagram of the data in the table.

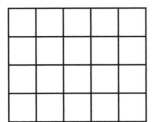  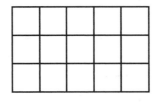  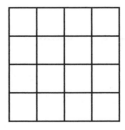

   b   Explain why that is the best grid to use.

_____

c   Complete this key by colouring each square a different colour.

Key

Sparrow ☐        Robin ☐        Pigeon ☐        Crow ☐

d   Colour the grid you have chosen to give a waffle diagram
     of the data in the table.

**Practice**

4   This Carroll diagram displays some information about
    learners' favourite sports and favourite colours.

|  |  | Favourite colour | |
|---|---|---|---|
|  |  | Red | Not red |
| **Favourite sport** | Football | Marcus<br><br>Rajiv | Sofia<br><br>Lou |
|  | Not football | Zara<br><br>Pablo | Arun<br><br>Sarah |

Complete this Venn diagram with information from the
Carroll diagram.

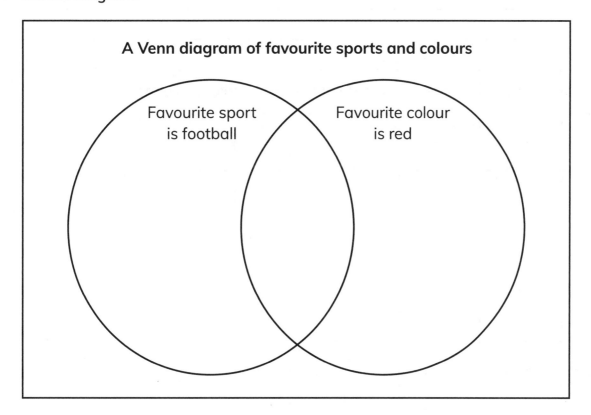

A Venn diagram of favourite sports and colours

Favourite sport is football

Favourite colour is red

5  Class 5 want to know how many pencils the children in their class have in their pencil cases.

This is how many each child has.

| 1 | 1 | 6 | 4 | 5 | 1 | 3 | 2 | 3 | 2 | 1 | 6 | 2 |
| 2 | 2 | 3 | 2 | 4 | 1 | 6 | 3 | 5 | 1 | 2 | 4 | 3 |

> **Tip**
>
> Always remember to give graphs and charts a title, and to label the axes.

a  Put the data about the number of pencils into the frequency table.

| Number of pencils | Tally | Frequency |
|---|---|---|
|  |  |  |
|  |  |  |
|  |  |  |
|  |  |  |
|  |  |  |
|  |  |  |

b  Draw a dot plot for the number of pencils in the children's pencil cases.

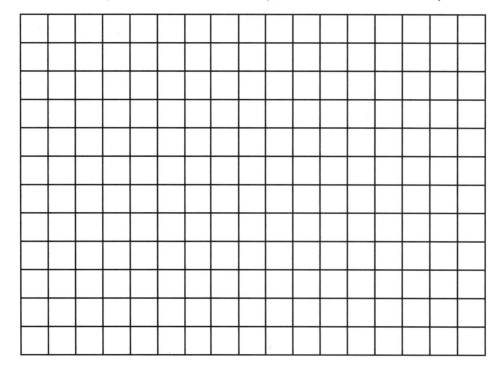

6   These two bar charts show the average monthly rainfall in two cities over one year.

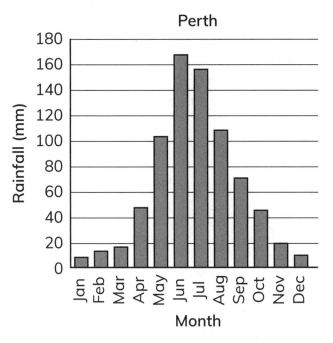

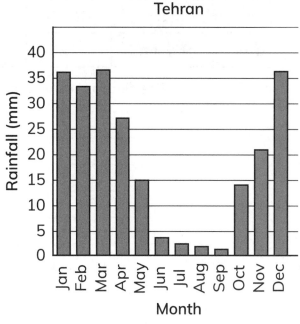

a   Describe the pattern in the bar chart of the rainfall in Perth.

_____

b   Describe the pattern in the bar chart of the rainfall in Tehran.

_____

c   Give three differences between the rainfall in Perth and in Tehran.

    1   _____

    2   _____

    3   _____

7 Some people voted for their favourite place.
Their votes are recorded in this table.

| Favourite place | Beach | City | Mountain | Forest | Ocean |
|---|---|---|---|---|---|
| Number of people | 12 | 1 | 1 | 4 | 6 |

a Draw a waffle diagram to represent the data in the table.

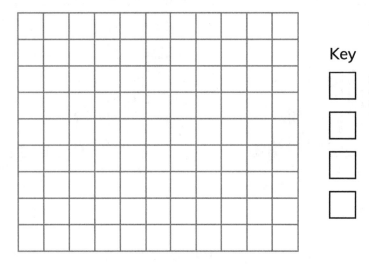

Key

b What percentage of the people voted for beach?

_____

c What fraction of the people voted for ocean?

_____

d Ask 24 people to choose their favourite place from beach, city, mountain, forest, ocean. Record their answers in the tally chart.

| Favourite place | Tally | Frequency |
|---|---|---|
| Beach | | |
| City | | |
| Mountain | | |
| Forest | | |
| Ocean | | |

Display your results in a waffle diagram.

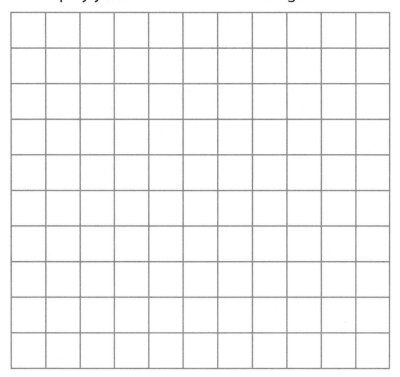

Key

e Describe how the data in the two waffle diagrams is similar and different.

_____

_____

_____

**Challenge**

8 a What is the average temperature in May?

_____

A bar chart to show the average temperatures at Cambridge Bay, Canada in degrees Celsius (°C)

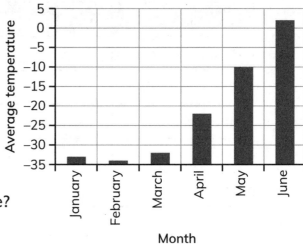

b What is the highest average temperature?

_____

c What is the lowest average temperature?

_____

d This is a table with temperatures for the next 6 months.

| Month | July | August | September | October | November | December |
|---|---|---|---|---|---|---|
| Temperature (°C) | 8 | 6 | −1 | −12 | −24 | −30 |

Label and draw a bar chart to show the temperatures for the whole year using the information from the table and the graph above.

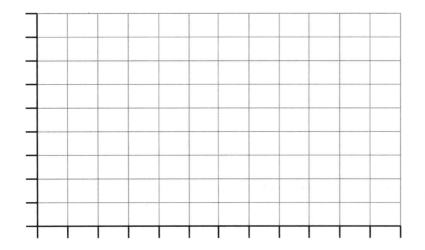

**Tip**

Look at the numbers that need to be recorded and choose a scale to fit.

 e Describe the pattern on the graph.

_____

_____

9  Lucas investigated the colour of sweets in packets.
He recorded the colour of 200 sweets.

a  Complete the table with the missing numbers of sweets,
fractions and percentages.

| Colour | Frequency | Fraction | Percentage |
|--------|-----------|----------|------------|
| Red | | $\frac{100}{200} = \frac{50}{100}$ | 50% |
| Yellow | 50 | $\frac{50}{200} = \frac{25}{100}$ | % |
| Green | 30 | | 15% |
| Orange | 20 | | % |

b  Display the percentages from the table in the waffle diagram.

Key

# > 12.2 Frequency diagrams and line graphs

**Worked example 2**

Sofia grew a plant from a seed. She measured her plant each week and recorded its height in a table.

Draw a line graph showing the data in this table.

| Time (weeks) | 1 | 2 | 3 | 4 | 5 | 6 |
|---|---|---|---|---|---|---|
| Height (cm) | 1 | 2 | 4 | 7 | 10 | 12 |

frequency diagram

line graph

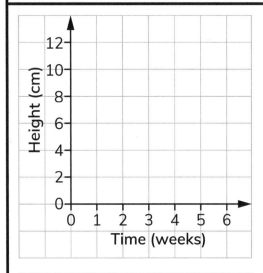

Label the x-axis with the time.

Label the y-axis with the height.

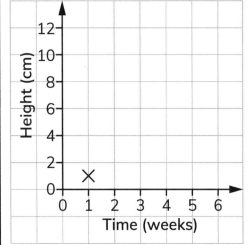

Find the first time on the x-axis, plot a point above that time at the height written in the table.

**Continued**

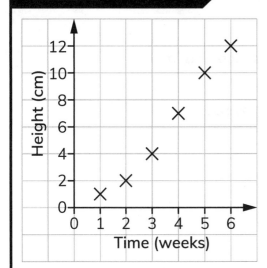

Plot the height of the plant for each time on the table.

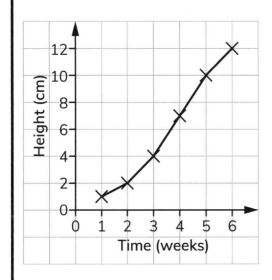

Join the plotted points in order with straight lines.

## Exercise 12.2

**Focus**

1   The mass of babies born in a hospital in one week is recorded in this frequency diagram.

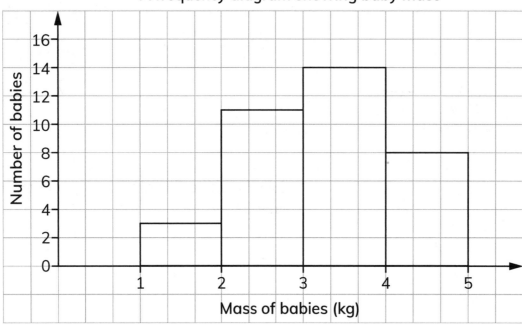

A frequency diagram showing baby mass

a   How many babies had a mass of more than 4 kg, but less than 5 kg?

_____

b   How many babies had a mass of less than 3 kg?

_____

c   How many babies were born in total in the hospital during the week?

_____

 d   Describe the shape of the graph.

The graph goes _____ , then back _____ .

2   Arun grew a plant from a seed. He measured his plant each week
    and recorded its height in a line graph.

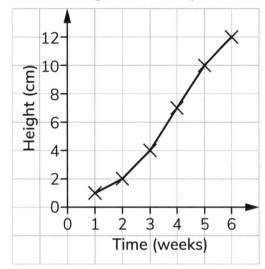

A line graph showing
the height of Arun's plant

a   How tall was Arun's plant at week 4?

    _____

b   When did Arun's plant reach 10 cm?

    _____

c   How much does Arun's plant grow between week 3 and week 5?

    _____

## Practice

3 One hundred 10-year-old children have their heights measured.
The results are shown in this frequency diagram.

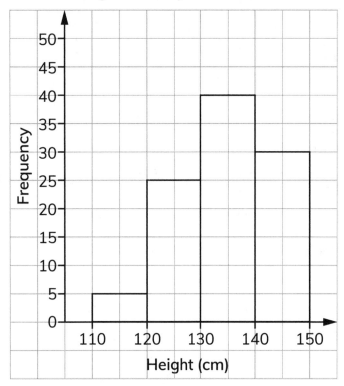

A frequency diagram showing
the heights of 10-year-old children

a How many children are shorter than 120 cm?

_____

b How many children are 130 cm or taller?

_____

c Ria says that the tallest child is 150 cm. Is that true or false?

_____

d How do you know?

_____

e John says that the shortest child is 110 cm. Explain why he might not be correct.

_____

4   Measure each of these plants to
    the nearest millimetre.

Day 1     Day 2     Day 3     Day 5     Day 6     Day 7

\_\_\_\_\_     \_\_\_\_\_     \_\_\_\_\_     \_\_\_\_\_     \_\_\_\_\_     \_\_\_\_\_

Plot the height of the plants on the graph. Join the points to make a line graph.

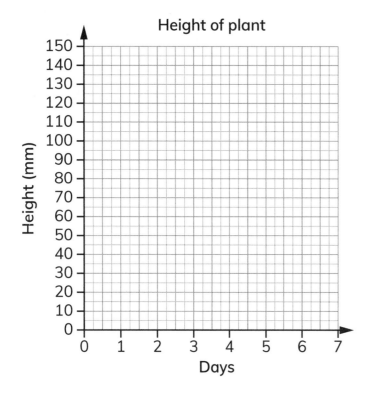

Height of plant

Use the information from the line graph to complete this sentence.

I estimate that the height of the plant on day 4 was _____ .

**Challenge**

5 The manager of the swimming pool wants to find out the
ages of people visiting the swimming pool.
These are the ages in years of the people the manager asks.

| 3 | 5 | 32 | 34 | 16 | 16 | 55 | 50 | 16 | 3 | 6 | 22 | 15 |
| 17 | 24 | 18 | 35 | 34 | 46 | 13 | 13 | 16 | 53 | 42 | 30 | 29 |

a Complete the frequency table of the ages.

| Age group (years) | Tally | Frequency |
|---|---|---|
| 0 to less than 10 | | |
| | | |
| | | |
| | | |
| | | |
| 50 to less than 60 | | |

b Draw a frequency diagram of the data in the table.

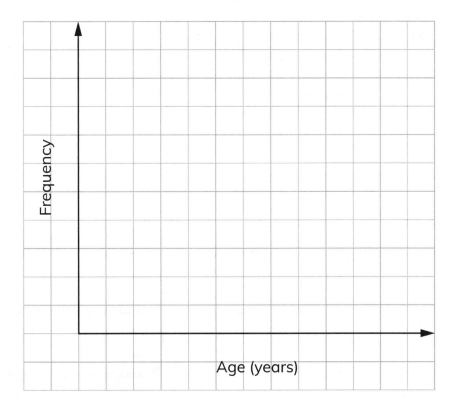

6   A group of children planted a stick in the ground.

They measured the length of its shadow six times in one day and drew a line graph of their results.

This is what the children said about the graph they made.

'The measurement at 2 p.m. was 8 cm longer than the shortest measurement.'

'The shadow at 1 p.m. was $\frac{1}{2}$ cm shorter than it had been at 11 a.m.'

'The difference in length between 10 a.m. and 11 a.m. was 5.5 cm.'

'The difference between the longest and shortest measurements was 15.5 cm.'

'The shadow was shortest at 12 o'clock.'

'The measurement at 11 a.m. was a square number.'

'The longest measurement was taken in the morning.'

'At 9 a.m. the length of the shadow was 21 cm.'

'The shadow gradually got shorter in the morning, then longer again in the afternoon.'

Use this information to draw their line graph.

Remember to label the axes and give the graph a title.

Use your graph to estimate how long the shadow was at half past 1.

**Tip**

Draw a table of times and shadow lengths, to start working out points on the graph.

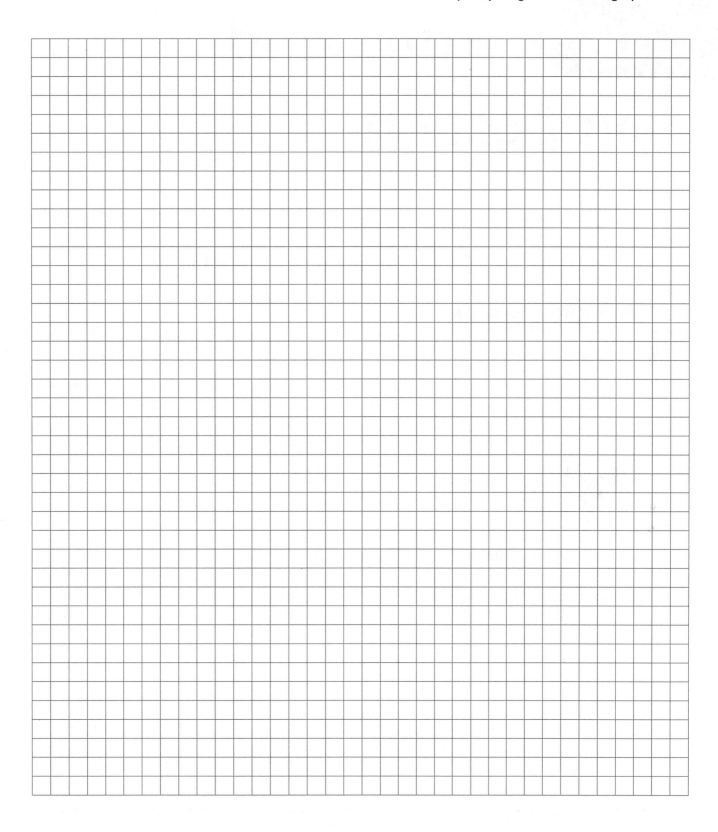

I estimate the shadow at half past 1 to be _____ .

# 13 ▶ Ratio and proportion

## > 13.1 Ratio and proportion

**Worked example 1**

A bag contains 3 black counters and 7 white counters.

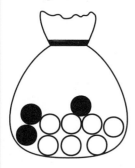

Complete these sentences.

**a** The ratio of white to black counters is _____ .

**b** The proportion of black counters is _____ .

| | | |
|---|---|---|
| **a** | The ratio of white to black counters is 7 : 3. | Remember that the ratio must be in order, white counters then black counters. |
| **b** | The proportion of black counters is $\frac{3}{10}$ or 30%. | The proportion is the number of black counters (3) out of the total number of counters (10) written as a fraction or a percentage. |

# Exercise 13.1

**Focus**

1   A farmer puts brown eggs and white eggs in a tray.

   a   What proportion of the eggs are white?

   _____

   b   What is the ratio of white eggs to brown eggs?

   white to brown = _____

   c   What is the ratio of brown eggs to white eggs?

   brown to white = _____

2   Steve is a decorator. He mixes paint to make new colours. He uses 1 can of blue paint and 2 cans of yellow paint to make green paint.

   He uses 3 cans of red paint and 4 cans of blue paint to make purple paint.

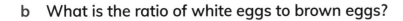
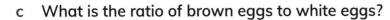

   a   What ratio of blue to yellow does Steve use to make green?

   blue to yellow = _____

   b   What ratio of blue to red does Steve use to make purple?

   blue to red = _____

   c   What proportion of purple paint is red?

   _____

   d   What proportion of green paint is yellow?

   _____

3   Sonya makes jewellery from grey and black beads.

a   What is the ratio of grey to black beads in her necklace?

b   Draw a necklace where $\frac{1}{4}$ of the beads are red.

c   Draw a different necklace where there are 2 pink beads for every 3 green beads.

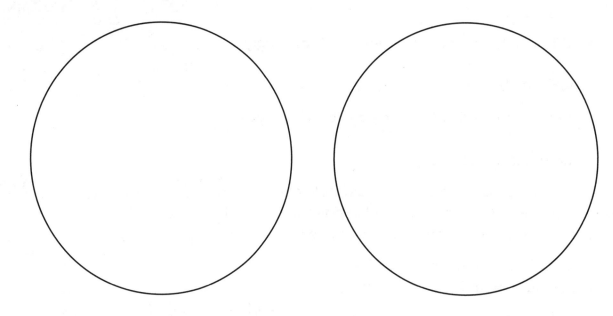

**Practice**

4   Here are ten shapes.

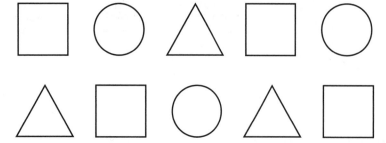

What proportion of the shapes are circles?

_____

5  Here is a pattern of shapes.

▢ ◯ ◯ ◯ ▢ ▢ ◯ ◯ ◯ ▢ ▢ ◯ ◯ ◯ ▢

Here are some statements about the pattern.
Some are correct and some are not correct.

A   There are 2 squares to every 3 circles

B   For every 1 square there are 3 circles

C   The ratio of squares to circles is 3 : 2

D   40% of the shapes are squares

E   The ratio of circles to squares is 3 : 2

F   $\frac{3}{4}$ of the shapes are circles

Write the letter of the statement in the correct place in the table.

| Correct | Not correct |
|---------|-------------|
|         |             |

6  Three children describe the same necklace and 1 child
describes a different necklace.

Abi says, '$\frac{1}{4}$ of the beads are white.'

Bruno says, 'For every 4 black beads there is 1 white bead.'

Conrad says, 'For every 1 white bead there are 3 black beads.'

Eva says, '$\frac{3}{4}$ of the beads are black.'

Who describes a different necklace? _____

Draw a necklace that three of the children describe.

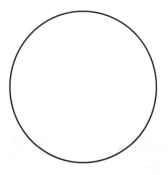

7 Here are two patterns and some statements.

Pattern A

Pattern B

| | |
|---|---|
| A | Ratio of triangles to circles is 1 : 4 |

| | |
|---|---|
| B | 1 in every 3 shapes is a triangle |

| | |
|---|---|
| C | 20% of the pattern is triangles |

| | |
|---|---|
| D | 1 out of 5 shapes is a triangle |

| | |
|---|---|
| E | Ratio of triangles to circles is 1 : 3 |

| | |
|---|---|
| F | $\frac{1}{5}$ of the pattern is triangles |

| | |
|---|---|
| G | 1 in every 4 shapes is a triangle |

| | |
|---|---|
| H | $\frac{1}{4}$ of the pattern is triangles |

| | |
|---|---|
| I | 25% of the pattern is triangles |

| | |
|---|---|
| J | 1 out of 4 shapes is a triangle |

Write the letter of each statement underneath the correct pattern.

| Pattern A | Pattern B |
|---|---|
| | |

Which statement have you not used? _____

**Challenge**

8   Four teams take part in a football tournament.
    These are the results.

| Wasps 3    Hornets 2 | Ants 1    Bees 1 |
|---|---|
| Hornets 1   Ants 3 | Bees 4    Wasps 2 |
| Bees 4    Hornets 1 | Wasps 6    Ants 2 |

Is each statement true or false?

a   In their match against the Bees, the Hornets scored $\frac{1}{4}$ of the goals.

    _____

b   Wasps scored more than half the total number of goals
    in each match they played.

    _____

c   In their match against the Bees, the Ants scored $\frac{1}{2}$ of the goals.

    _____

9 These tile patterns should all have 3 grey tiles for every
2 black tiles. One tile is not coloured.

A 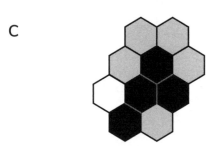 B

C  D

a What colour should the missing tiles be?

A _____ B _____ C _____ D _____

b What proportion of the tiles in the completed patterns are grey?

_____

c What proportion of the tiles in the completed patterns are black?

_____

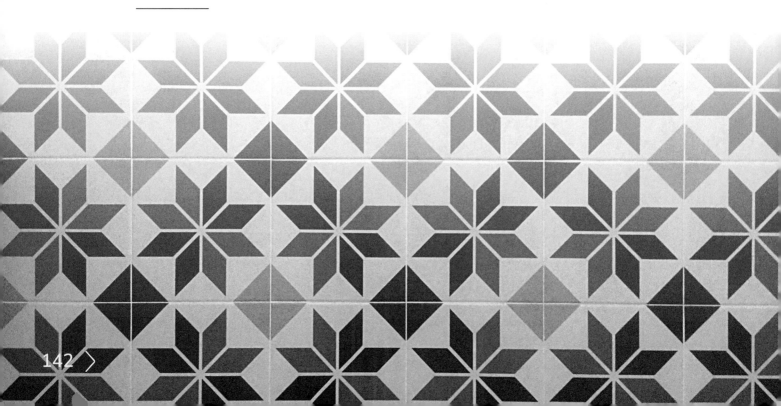

10  Here is a recipe for making fruit salad.

> **Fruit salad**
>
> 2 grapefruit
>
> 4 oranges
>
> 4 apricots
>
> Eat with a spoonful of honey.

a   What is the ratio of grapefruit : orange : apricot?

_____

b   What is the ratio of orange : apricot : grapefruit?

_____

c   What proportion of the fruit is orange?
Write your answer as a fraction and a percentage.

_____

d   What proportion of the fruit is grapefruit?
Write your answer as a fraction and a percentage.

_____

11  Zara says, 'My diagram shows 1 in every 3 shapes is a triangle.'

△ ◯ ◯ ◯ △ ◯ ◯ ◯ △ ◯ ◯ ◯

Explain why Zara might think she is correct.

What should Zara have written?

_____

_____

_____

# 14 ▶ Area and perimeter

## ❯ 14.1 Area and perimeter

**Worked example 1**

What is the area of this shape?

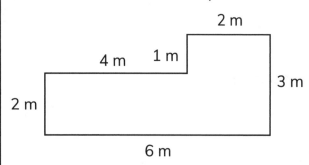

| area |
|------|
| perimeter |

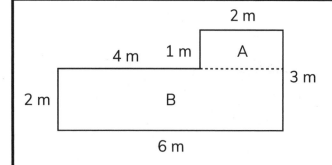

Divide the shape into rectangles.

Area of rectangle A = 2 × 1 = 2 m$^2$

Area of rectangle B = 6 × 2 = 12 m$^2$

2 m$^2$ + 12 m$^2$ = 14 m$^2$

Calculate the area of each rectangle.

Find the total area by adding together the areas of the rectangles.

**Answer:** The area of the shape is 14 m$^2$.

# Exercise 14.1

**Focus**

1   Draw one straight line through each shape to divide it into
    two rectangles.

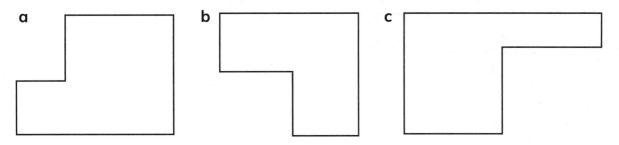

a          b          c

2   Label all the sides with the missing lengths.

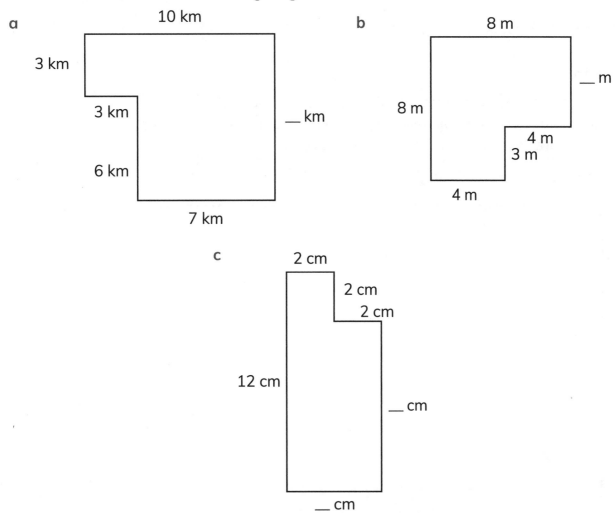

3   Work out the total area of this shape.

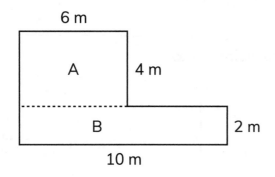

The area of rectangle A is _____ .

The area of rectangle B is _____ .

The total area is _____ .

**Practice**

4   Marcus says that the number of centimetres around the perimeter of a rectangle will always be greater than the number of square centimetres in the rectangle's area.

Draw and label a rectangle to show that Marcus is wrong.

5 Work out the perimeter and area of each square.

a    Perimeter =          Area =

3 m

_____          _____

b   Perimeter =          Area =

4 m

_____          _____

c   Perimeter =          Area =

5 m

_____          _____

6 Work out the perimeter and area of this shape.

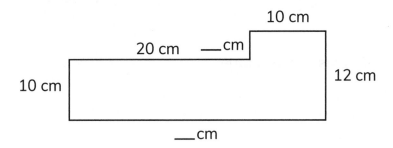

Perimeter = _____          Area = _____

7  a  Estimate the perimeter and area of this shape without measuring.

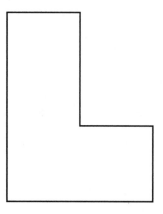

I estimate the area of the shape is _____ cm$^2$.

I estimate the perimeter of the shape is _____ cm.

b  Measure the shape and work out its area and perimeter.

Area = _____

Perimeter = _____

**Challenge**

8  Label the missing lengths on the sides of this shape.

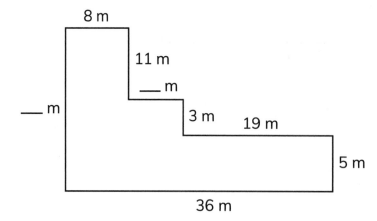

9    Draw a rectangle that has:

a    An area of 6 cm$^2$ and a perimeter
     of 14 cm.

**Tip**

You could try drawing different
rectangles with an area of 6 cm$^2$ until you
find one that has a perimeter of 14 cm.

b    An area of 12 cm$^2$ and a perimeter of 14 cm.

c   An area of 24 cm$^2$ and a perimeter of 22 cm.

10 Label the measurements that are missing from the shape.

Divide this shape into rectangles.

Find the total area of the shape.

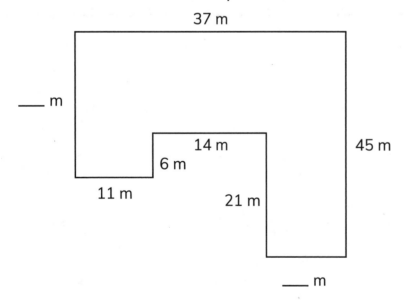

Total area = _____

# 15 ▶ Multiplying and dividing fractions and decimals

## ❭ 15.1 Multiplying and dividing fractions

**Worked example 1**

Draw a diagram to show $\frac{1}{6} \div 2$.

> repeated addition
>
> unit fraction

Think about the size of your answer.

Will it be larger or smaller than $\frac{1}{6}$?

Draw a diagram divided into 6 equal parts.

Shade $\frac{1}{6}$.

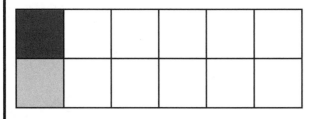

Divide the diagram into 2 equal parts.

Find the size of $\frac{1}{6}$ divided by 2.

**Answer:**

$\frac{1}{6} \div 2 = \frac{1}{12}$

# Exercise 15.1

**Focus**

1   Complete the number line to show $\frac{1}{4} \times 5$.

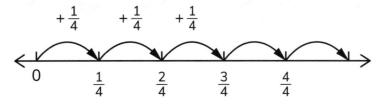

$\frac{1}{4} \times 5 = \boxed{\phantom{00}}$

2   Complete the diagram to show $\frac{1}{8} \times 7$.

$\frac{1}{8} \times 7 = \boxed{\phantom{00}}$

3   Complete the diagram to show $\frac{1}{9} \div 3$.

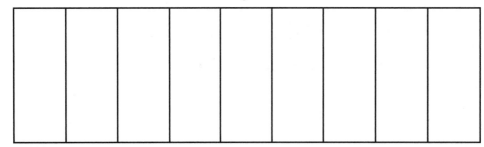

$\frac{1}{9} \div 3 = \boxed{\phantom{00}}$

4   Complete the calculation that is shown by the diagram.

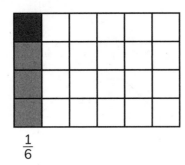

$\frac{1}{6} \div \boxed{\phantom{0}} = \boxed{\dfrac{\phantom{00}}{\phantom{00}}}$

## Practice

5   Calculate.

a   $\frac{1}{3} \times 5$

b   $\frac{1}{4} \div 3$

c   $\frac{1}{5} \times 7$

_____        _____        _____

6   Marcus has $\frac{1}{2}$ of a bottle of fruit juice.

He divides it equally between three glasses.

What fraction of the bottle is in each glass?

_____

7   This fraction model shows 6 whole units.

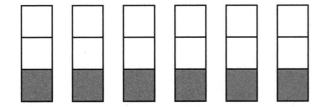

Tick (✓) the number sentence that represents the amount that is shaded.

$6 \times \frac{1}{2}$ ☐          $6 \times \frac{1}{3}$ ☐

$3 \times \frac{1}{6}$ ☐          $3 \times \frac{1}{2}$ ☐

8   Work out the answer to each question to help you find your way through the maze.

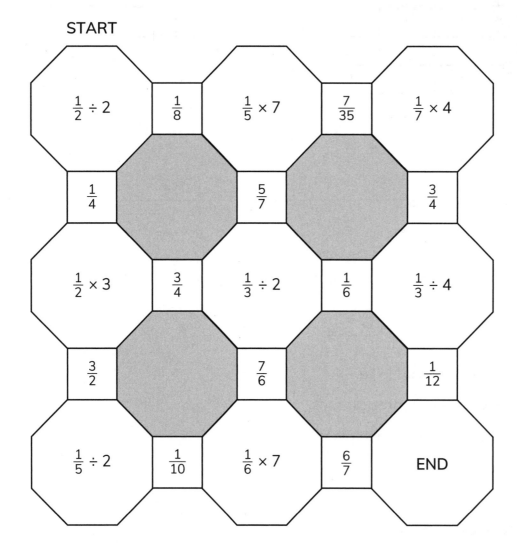

**Challenge**

9   Write the missing fractions.

a   $\boxed{\phantom{xx}} \times 5 = \dfrac{5}{6}$

b   $\boxed{\phantom{xx}} \times 8 = \dfrac{8}{9}$

**10** Arun multiplies a fraction by a whole number.

He writes

$$\frac{1}{6} \times 7 = \frac{7}{42}$$

Explain what Arun has done wrong, then correct his answer.

_____

_____

**11** Sofia has $\frac{1}{4}$ of a cake.

She divides the cake into three pieces and eats one of the pieces.

What fraction of Sofia's cake is left?

Show your working.

_____

_____

**12** Jodi has 2 metres of string.

She uses $\frac{1}{5}$ of a metre to make a bracelet.

Jodi makes 6 bracelets.

How much string is left?

_____

# > 15.2 Multiplying a decimal and a whole number

decimal

decimal place

decimal point

**Worked example 2**

Calculate 3.4 × 6

Estimate: 3 × 6 = 18

Always start with an estimate.

|   | 3 • | 4 |
|---|---|---|
| × |   | 6 |
|   | • | 4 |
|   | 2 |   |

One possible method is to write the calculation in columns.

Make sure the decimal point in the answer is in line with the decimal point in the number.

Carry out the multiplication in the same way as you do for whole numbers. In this case:

|   | 3 • | 4 |
|---|---|---|
| × |   | 6 |
| 2 | 0 • | 4 |
|   | 2 |   |

- 0.4 × 6 = 2.4. Place the digit 4 in the tenths column and carry the digit 2 to the ones column.

- 3 × 6 = 18. Add the 2 that was carried to give 20. Place the digit 0 in the ones column and the digit 2 in the tens column.

Check that your answer is close to your estimate.

**Answer:** Estimate 3 × 6 = 18 and 4 × 6 = 24 so the answer will be between 18 and 24.

3.4 × 6 = 20.4

# Exercise 15.2

## Focus

**Tip**

Remember to estimate before you calculate.

1 Conrad counts in steps of 0.2.

He says, 'zero-point-two, zero-point-four, ...'

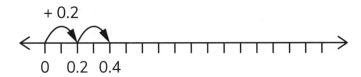

+ 0.2

0   0.2  0.4

He continues counting to calculate $7 \times 0.2$.

What is the answer?

_____

2 Complete these calculations.

a
$0.7 \times 6$

$7 \div 10 \qquad \times \boxed{\phantom{0}}$

$= 7 \times \boxed{\phantom{0}} \div 10$

$= \boxed{\phantom{0}} \div 10$

$= \boxed{\phantom{0}}$

b
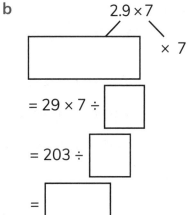

$2.9 \times 7$

$\boxed{\phantom{000}} \qquad \times 7$

$= 29 \times 7 \div \boxed{\phantom{0}}$

$= 203 \div \boxed{\phantom{0}}$

$= \boxed{\phantom{0}}$

3 Zara spills ink on her work. Work out what the hidden digit is in each calculation.

a $0.7 \times 5 = 3.$ ⬛ _____

b $0.9 \times 8 =$ ⬛ $.2$ _____

c $0.$ ⬛ $\times 8 = 5.6$ _____

**Practice**

4  Complete these calculations.

a

|     | 1 • 2 |
| :-: | :-: |
| ×   | 4   |
|     |     |

b

|     | 6 • 3 |
| :-: | :-: |
| ×   | 5   |
|     |     |

c

|     | 7 • 6 |
| :-: | :-: |
| ×   | 8   |
|     |     |

5  What is the product of 8.3 and 7?

6  Draw a line from each calculation to the correct description for the answer.

$1.8 \times 6$

$2.4 \times 4$          Answer less than 10

$1.8 \times 5$          Answer equal to 10

$2.5 \times 4$          Answer more than 10

**Challenge**

7  Look at these four calculations.

One is **wrong**.

| $9.5 \times 3 = 28.5$ | $3.9 \times 9 = 35.1$ | $2.6 \times 4 = 12.4$ | $4.2 \times 6 = 25.2$ |

Put a cross (✗) through the incorrect calculation without finding the answer.
Explain how you did it.

8  Use the digits 4, 5 and 6 to make this calculation correct.

$$\boxed{\phantom{0}} . \boxed{\phantom{0}} \times \boxed{\phantom{0}} = 26$$

9  Sofia decorates 7 cards with ribbon.

She uses 22.5 centimetres on each card.

How many centimetres of ribbon does Sofia use?

_____ cm

10  Arun is thinking of a number.

He says, 'If I divide my number by 6 the answer is 17.5.'

What number is Arun thinking of?

_____

11  Zina runs 1.6 kilometres every day for a week.

Sally runs 1.9 kilometres each day for 6 days.

Who runs the greater distance?

Explain your answer.

_____

_____

# 16 ▶ Time

## > 16.1 Time intervals and time zones

## Exercise 16.1

**Focus**

> time interval
>
> time zone
>
> Universal Time (UT)

 1 Draw a ring around the amount of time to correctly complete each sentence.

  a   0.5 minutes is the same as:

   30 seconds        5 seconds        50 seconds

  b   0.5 hours is the same as:

   5 minutes        30 seconds        30 minutes

  c   1.5 days is the same as:

   1 day and 5 hours        1 day and 12 hours        1 day and 15 hours

d 120 minutes is the same as:

3 hours                    12 hours                    2 hours

e 90 seconds is the same as:

1.5 minutes                9 minutes                   2 minutes

2 Marco runs every day.

a On Monday he started his run at 09:45 and ran for 30 minutes. What time did he finish his run?

_____

b On Tuesday he started his run at 10:50 and ran for 20 minutes. What time did he finish his run?

_____

c On Wednesday he started his run at 09:50 and finished his run at 10:10. How long did he run for?

_____

d On Thursday he started his run at 10:25 and finished his run at 11:15. How long did he run for?

_____

e   On Friday he started his run at 09:20 and finished his run at 10:30. How long did he run for?

_____

3   Complete the sentence and draw hands on Sofia's clock to show the time where she is.

08:45

Hi Sofia, what time is it where you are?

Hi Zara, my time is 5 hours ahead of you. It is

_____

here.

## Practice

4  a  Lina did 5 activities. She timed how long each activity took.
      Draw lines between the activities and the times to show
      how long you think each activity took.

| | |
|---|---|
| She wrote a chapter of a story. | 0.5 seconds |
| She swam one width of a swimming pool. | 2 seconds |
| She wrote her name. | 3 minutes |
| She picked up a pencil. | 0.5 minutes |
| She boiled a kettle. | 0.5 hours |

   b  Write the activities in order from the shortest to the longest time.

   _____

   _____

   _____

   _____

5   Tom takes part in a game where he solves puzzles in each room before he can move to the next room.

The clock in each room shows the time that Tom entered that room.

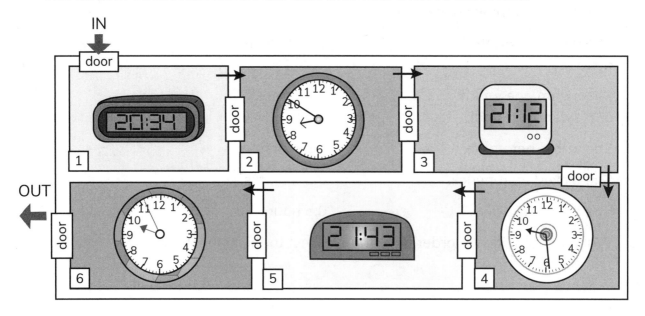

How long did Tom spend in each room?

Room 1: _____          Room 2: _____

Room 3: _____          Room 4: _____

Room 5: _____

Tom took 1 hour and 15 minutes to complete the puzzle in Room 6.
At what time did Tom leave Room 6?

_____

6   a   How many time zones are there in the world?

There are _____ time zones.

b   Name two countries that have more than one time zone.

_____ and _____ have more than one time zone.

> **Tip**
>
> You could find the answer on a world map or with an internet search.

7   Four friends, Adam, Jess, Meena and Josh, live in different time zones. Draw lines to show which clock belongs to each friend.

Clues:

- The clock in Meena's home shows an earlier time than the clock in Jess' home.

- Jess' clock shows a time that is 2 hours ahead of Adam's time.

- Adam's time is ahead of Josh's but behind Meena's.

| Adam | Jess | Meena | Josh |

**Challenge**

8  a  Luca accidentally put his bus timetable in the washing machine!
Every bus takes the same amount of time to reach the destinations.
Work out the times that have been washed away.

|  | Bus A | Bus B | Bus C | Bus D |
|---|---|---|---|---|
| Village | 11:51 | 12:48 |  | 15:42 |
| Town | 12:08 |  |  |  |
| City | 12:32 |  | 14:36 | 23 |
| Harbour | 12:47 | 13: | 14:51 | 16:38 |

b  Think about how you solved this problem. Include:

• Where did you start? Why?

• What calculations did you do?

• How did you check your solutions?

Write how you can improve how you solve problems like this.

_____

_____

_____

9  These clocks show the times in different cities.

Lima
(05:51)

São Paulo
(07:51)

Cape Town
(12:51)

Chennai
(15:21)

Tokyo
(19:51)

Adelaide
(20:21)

This is a table to show the time difference between cities.

| | | | | | |
|---|---|---|---|---|---|
| Lima | | | | | |
| | São Paulo | | | | |
| | | Cape Town | | | |
| | | | Chennai | | |
| 14 hours | | | | Tokyo | |
| | | | | | Adelaide |

The table shows that there is a 14 hour time difference between Lima and Tokyo.

Complete the table showing the time difference between the different cities using the clocks.

10  Use the table and clocks from question 9 to help you calculate the day and time in:

a   Cape Town if it is 08:13 on Wednesday in Lima

_____

b   Chennai if it is 10.37 p.m. on Saturday in Cape Town

_____

c   Sao Paulo if it is 17:28 on Tuesday in Tokyo

_____

d   Lima if it is 09.09 a.m. on Friday in Adelaide.

_____

# 17 ▶ Number and the laws of arithmetic

## > 17.1 The laws of arithmetic

### Worked example 1

Are the following statements true or false?

a   $7 \times 6 = 6 \times 7$        b   $8 + 2 \times 8 = 80$

Explain your answers.

| associative law | decompose |
| commutative law | distributive law |
| | regroup |

**Answers:**

a   True.

The commutative law states that when two numbers are added or multiplied, you can do the calculation in any order.

b   False.

The learner has added 8 and 2 to give 10, then multiplied by 8.
The order of operations is multiplication before addition, so the answer is $8 + 16 = 24$, not 80.

## Exercise 17.1

**Focus**

1   Look at each number sentence.

Write true or false for each one.

a   $8 \times 2 = 2 \times 8$ _____

b   $28 \div 4 = 4 \div 28$ _____

c   $5 \times 9 \times 2 = 5 \times 2 \times 9$ _____

2   Write the missing number.

$13 \times 36 = 13 \times \boxed{\phantom{0}} \times 9$

3   Use single digits to complete this number sentence.

$25 \times 15 = \boxed{\phantom{0}} \times \boxed{\phantom{0}} \times \boxed{\phantom{0}} \times \boxed{\phantom{0}}$

4   Calculate.

a   $4 + 7 \times 6 =$ _____

b   $12 - 2 \times 6 =$ _____

c   $14 + 6 \div 3 =$ _____

**Practice**

5   Complete these calculations.

a   $7 \times 5 \times 2 = 5 \times \boxed{\phantom{0}} \times 7$

$= \boxed{\phantom{0}} \times 7$

$= \boxed{\phantom{0}}$

b

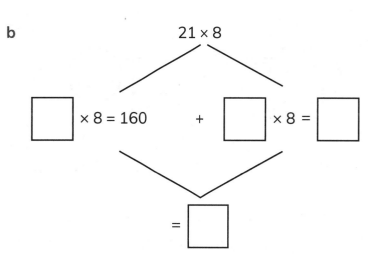

6   Sofia knows that $48 \times 20 = 960$.

Show how she can use this fact to calculate $48 \times 19$.

_____

_____

7 Use numbers and operation signs from the box to make three calculations giving different answers.

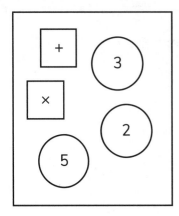

You can only use each number once in each calculation, but you can use the same operation sign more than once.

◯ ▢ ◯ ▢ ◯ = _____

◯ ▢ ◯ ▢ ◯ = _____

◯ ▢ ◯ ▢ ◯ = _____

8 Use +, −, ×, ÷ to complete these number sentences.

Example: 3 ☐×☐ 4 ☐−☐ 6 = 6

a 8 ☐ 12 ☐ 3 = 12     b 5 ☐ 9 ☐ 3 = 42

c 7 ☐ 6 ☐ 3 = 9     d 10 ☐ 2 ☐ 2 = 3

9 Ali, Bashir, Petra and Tara calculate 25 × 8 using different methods.

Which method do you prefer?
You must explain the advantages of your chosen method.

Ali's method

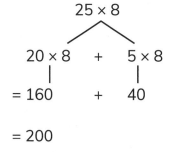

25 × 8

20 × 8    +    5 × 8

= 160    +    40

= 200

Bashir's method

25 × 8 = 5 × 5 × 8

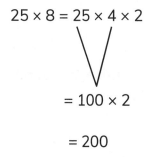

= 5 × 40

= 200

Petra's method

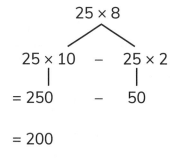

25 × 8

25 × 10    −    25 × 2

= 250    −    50

= 200

Tara's method

25 × 8 = 25 × 4 × 2

= 100 × 2

= 200

_____

_____

**Challenge**

10 Explain whether each calculation will give an answer equal
to the product of 12 and 8.

a   $3 \times 4 \times 8$

_____

_____

b   $12 \times 4 \times 2$

_____

_____

c   $2 + 10 \times 8$

_____

_____

11 Use the distributive law to help you work out these calculations.
Show your working.

a   $39 \times 7$

_____

_____

b   $38 \times 8$

_____

_____

c   $29 \times 7$

_____

_____

**12** Use the associative law to help you work out these calculations. Show your working.

a   5 × 17 × 4

_____

_____

b   50 × 12 × 4

_____

_____

c   25 × 19 × 4

_____

_____

**13** Write the missing numbers.

a   $3 \times \boxed{\phantom{0}} + 4 = 19$

b   $4 \times 8 - \boxed{\phantom{0}} = 29$

c   $6 + 7 \times \boxed{\phantom{0}} = 41$

d   $16 \div \boxed{\phantom{0}} - 3 = 1$

e   $3 \times \boxed{\phantom{0}} - 6 = 18$

f   $13 - 12 \div \boxed{\phantom{0}} = 9$

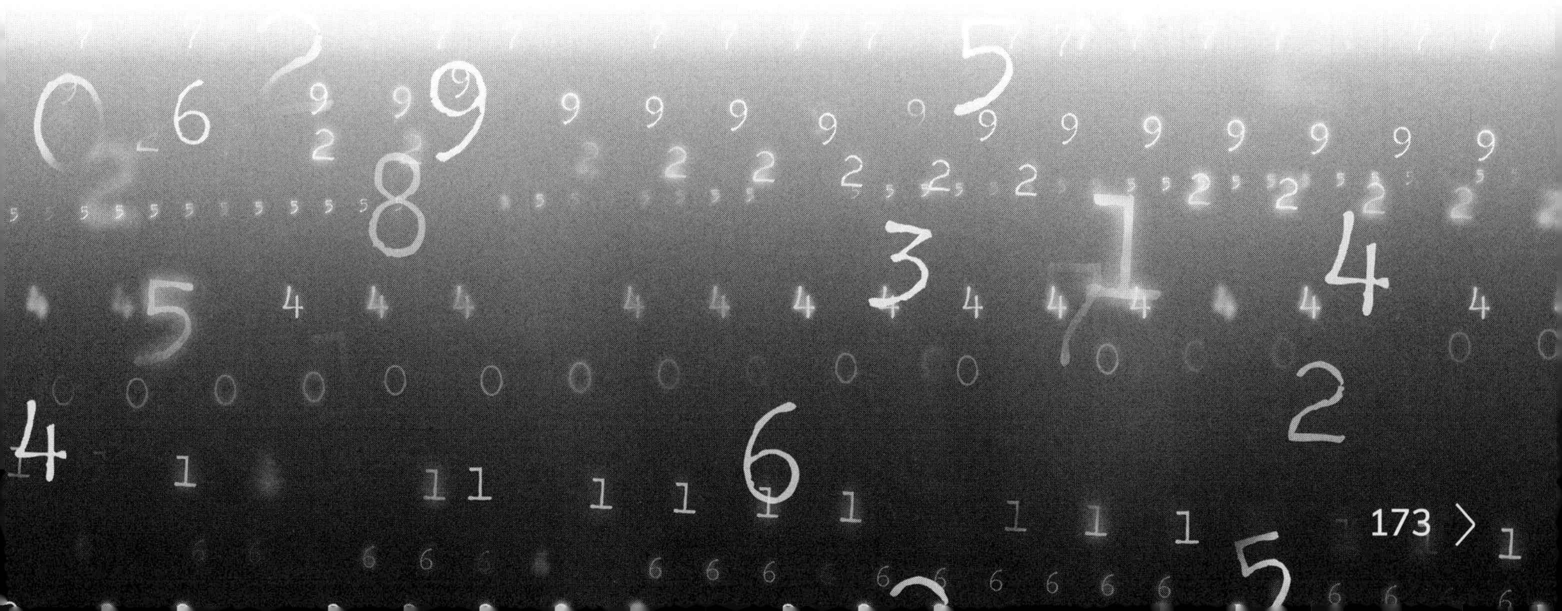

# 18 ▶ Position and direction

## > 18.1 Coordinates and translation

**Worked example 1**

The coordinates of three vertices of a rectangle are (3, 1), (4, 1) and (3, 5). What are the coordinates of the fourth vertex?

A rectangle has four sides and four vertices. It has two pairs of opposite equal parallel sides and four right angles.

Check the definition of a rectangle.

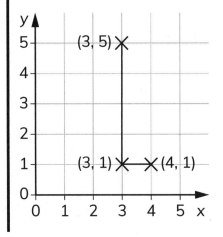

Plot the coordinates on a grid.
Join the points with straight lines.

**Continued**

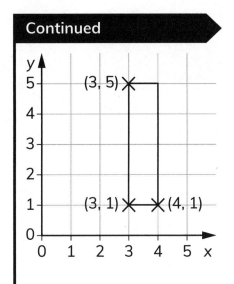

The other two sides must make right angles with the first sides. For this question, each line can be drawn in only one direction. Draw the other two sides.

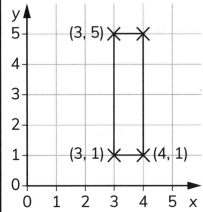

The fourth vertex is where the sides of the rectangle meet.

**Answer:** The fourth vertex has coordinates (4, 5).

# Exercise 18.1

**Focus**

1   Write the coordinates that are inside the circle on the grid.

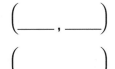      ( ____ , ____ )

( ____ , ____ )   ( ____ , ____ )   ( ____ , ____ )

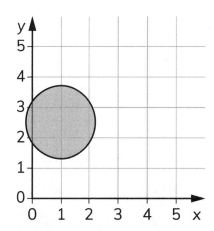

2  a  Draw two lines to complete the square on the grid.

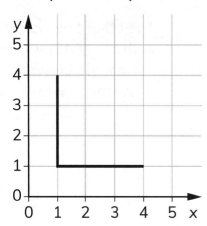

b  Two of the coordinates at the vertices of the square are
   (1, 1) and (1, 4). What are coordinates of the other two vertices?

   (___ , ___)    (___ , ___)

3  Draw a ring around the numbers and words that describe the translation
   from shape A to shape B.

a
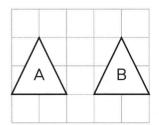

1 / 2 / 3 squares right / left / up / down

b
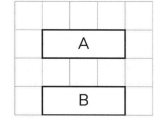

1 / 2 / 3 squares right / left / up / down

c
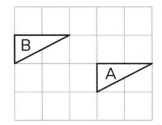

1 / 2 / 3 squares right / left / up / down

and

1 / 2 / 3 squares right / left / up / down

## Practice

4   The coordinates of three vertices of a rectangle are
    (0, 1), (0, 4) and (4, 4).

    What are the coordinates of the fourth vertex of the rectangle?

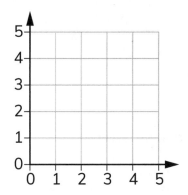

_____

5   A cross is marked at point (50, 50) on the grid.
    Estimate the coordinates of points A, B and C.

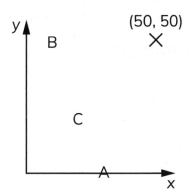

(50, 50)

    a   A is approximately       (____ , ____)

    b   B is approximately       (____ , ____)

    c   C is approximately       (____ , ____)

6  Look at this picture of a shape that has been translated.

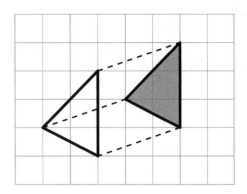

Draw a ring around **True** or **False** for each statement about translating shapes.

Translated shapes travel in a straight line.          True / False

A shape gets larger when it is translated.          True / False

A shape rotates when it is translated.          True / False

The lines joining the vertices of the first
shape to the translated shape are parallel.          True / False

7  Translate each shape according to the instructions.

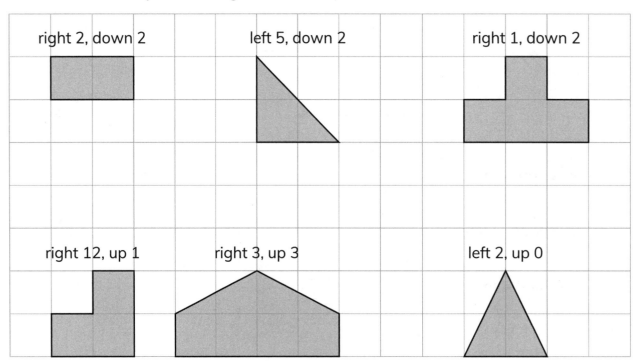

**Challenge**

8   A farmer keeps his sheep safe by putting them no more than 20 metres away from the farmhouse and not too close to the river or the road.

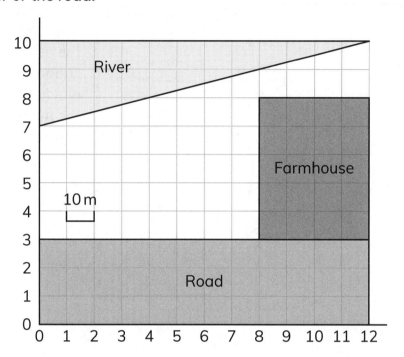

> **Tip**
>
> Use the scale on the map to work out distances.

Write the coordinates for five points where the sheep will be safest.

_____

_____

9   Two vertices of an isosceles triangle are at (2, 2) and (4, 2). Find the coordinates for the 9 possible positions of the third vertex on this grid.

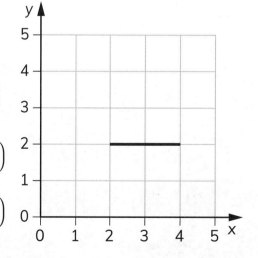

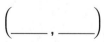  

**10** Translate the triangle four times to pass through the maze.

After each translation, the triangle should land within the maze.

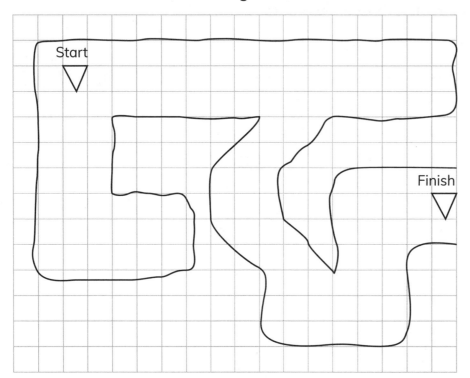

**Tip**

Write your directions using the number of squares right or left, then the number of squares up or down for each translation.

1 _____    2 _____

3 _____    4 _____

# ⟩ Acknowledgements

It takes a number of people to put together a new series of resources and their comments, support and encouragement have been really important to us.

From Mary Wood: With thanks to Katherine Bird, my editor, for her wise words, to my son, David for his willingness to talk mathematics and respond to my IT needs and to my husband, Norman, for being there when it was tough going.

From Emma Low: With thanks to Katherine and Caroline for their indispensable ideas and feedback, and also to Andy and our daughters Natasha, Jessica and Phoebe for their love and support and occasional very helpful puzzle and problem testing.

From Cambridge University Press: We would like to thank the following people: Katherine Bird and Suzanne Thurston for their support for the authors; Lynne McClure for her feedback and comments on early sections of the manuscript; Thomas Carter, Caroline Walton, Laura Collins, Charlotte Griggs, Gabby Martin, Elizabeth Scurfield, Berenice Howard-Smith, Zohir Naciri, Emma McCrea and Eddie Rippeth as part of the team at Cambridge preparing the resources. We would also like to particularly thank all of the anonymous reviewers for their time and comments on the manuscript and as part of the endorsement process.

*The authors and publishers acknowledge the following sources of copyright material and are grateful for the permissions granted. While every effort has been made, it has not always been possible to identify the sources of all the material used, or to trace all copyright holders. If any omissions are brought to our notice, we will be happy to include the appropriate acknowledgements on reprinting.*

*Thanks to the following for permission to reproduce images:*

Cover illustration: Pablo Gallego (Beehive Illustration)

Photos: Sir Francis Canker Photography/GI; Tobias Titz/GI; Melinda Podor/GI; Kelvin Murray/GI; Sean Gladwell/GI; Diane Labombarbe/GI; spooh/GI; fitri iskandar zakariah/GI; Image Soure/GI; yuanyuan yan/GI; Peter Dazeley/GI; Torsten Albrecht/EyeEm/GI; ROBERT BROOK/SCIENCE PHOTO LIBRARY/GI; kaanates/GI; Thegoodly/GI; Wathanyu Kanthawong / EyeEm/GI; R. Tsubin/GI; Tim Grist Photography/GI; Tim Hall/GI; Mai Tsugihara/GI; Photograph by Emma Johnson/GI; CAP53/GI;

Cathy Scola/GI; Jose A. Bernat Bacete/GI; Mint Images/GI; the_burtons/GI; Phat'hn Sakdi Skul Phanthu/EyeEm/GI; Oscark Alvarez/EyeEm; Christina Hanck/GI; porcorex/GI; East Road/Ascent Xmedia/GI; leminuit/GI; David Prahl/EyeEm/GI; Cosmo Condina/GI; Grant Faint/GI; Tetra Images/GI; kevinjeon00/GI

GI = Getty Images